LIGHT
THEIR FIRE

**GUIDELINES FOR EFFECTIVELY
TEACHING ADULTS**

TWENTY-NINE MATCHES INCLUDED

Piedmont Baptist College and Graduate School
420 South Broad Street • Winston-Salem, NC 27101 • www.pbc.edu

LEONARD ALLRED, PH.D.

Light Their Fire
Guidelines For Effectively Teaching Adults
Twenty-Nine Matches Included

ISBN 978-0-9708261-2-1

(c) 2007
Piedmont Baptist College Press
A department of Piedmont Baptist College and Graduate School
Winston-Salem, NC

Printed in U.S.A.
All rights reserved.

No part of this work may be copied, photocopied, transmitted, recorded, reproduced or stored in any electronic retrieval system, whether by mechanical or electronic means except by the express written consent of the publisher. Publisher reserves world rights in all languages and formats.

DEDICATION

To my dear wife,
God's wonderful gift to me
and
my greatest cheerleader

ACKNOWLEDGMENTS

Years ago, I came across some great advice: "Never be ashamed to borrow brains." As I checked my meager supply of this commodity, it quickly became apparent that I needed to borrow all that I could find! So, in thinking of those I might be able to tap for help in writing and editing this book, I soon realized I needed some input from a variety of sources. First of all, I needed individuals who were themselves prolific readers and had thereby developed the ability to spot a book that might have a chance to reach a publisher's desk one day. My first choice was my dear wife and sweetheart, who through the years has devoured a ton of books. Thank you, Honey, for all your kind words of encouragement and being willing to relinquish some of our time together so I could get this thing done.

Our older daughter, Ruth, apparently "inherited" some of her Mom's love for reading, and came through beautifully with some excellent research and helpful suggestions as to how the text could be more finely tuned. She and Kim, our other daughter, have been a source of continuing prayer support and encouragement during this venture.

Roger Barnes, teaching assistant, library associate, and valued friend, here at Piedmont Baptist College, demonstrated again his servant heart by being willing to devote a generous amount of his time to read the manuscript, check for historical accuracy of dates and events, and provide some great anecdotes. Thanks, Roger, for being there for me.

I felt it was also imperative to get some feedback from someone who would know if the stuff in this book would actually work "in the trenches" while teaching adults in a Sunday School class. My first choice here was Lynn Greear, godly layman, successful businessman, and faithful teacher for years. Thank you also, Lynn, for carving out a large chunk of time from your busy schedule to read this twice and make valuable suggestions.

Finally, I am extremely indebted to Dr. Beth Ashburn, Vice-President of Academics, and Mrs. Sandra Perkins, English teacher, here at the College. Without their willingness to spend enormous amounts of their time checking format, grammar, and composition, this book would have never become a reality. A very special word of thanks to you, Beth and Sandra.

CONTENTS

INTRODUCTION

MATCHES

1. Be a consistent model
2. Be filled with the Spirit
3. Pray! Pray! Pray!
4. Love your adults and demonstrate it
5. Keep yourself as physically attractive as possible
6. Be sure you are teaching - not just talking
7. Remember whom you are teaching
8. Learn and use their names
9. Prepare well for each lesson
10. Make a lesson plan
11. Grab and keep their attention
12. Show them why they need the material you are teaching them
13. Invite their input in selecting topics for study
14. Help them apply God's truths to their lives
15. Be sure you are communicating
16. Use a variety of teaching methods
17. Occasionally assign names of your adults, who are present, to the characters you use in a role play or case study
18. Get your adults involved in the lesson
19. Look them in the eye
20. Use illustrations throughout your lesson
21. Schedule surgery for that monotone
22. Use plenty of positive reinforcement

23. Sprinkle in some humor
24. Terminate those mannerisms
25. Be enthusiastic
26. Watch your body language!
27. Make your classroom "user friendly"
28. Keep up with breaking news
29. Maintain a Christian attitude when others disagree with you

APPENDIX A - SAMPLE PRAYER LIST
APPENDIX B - SAMPLE LESSON PLAN (FORMAT)
APPENDIX C - SAMPLE LESSON PLAN (COMPLETED)
APPENDIX D - HANDOUT: FIVE SINS AGAINST THE SPIRIT

INTRODUCTION

Write another evangelical book on the principles and methods of teaching adults? I kept telling myself, "You've gotta be kidding." What could I possibly add to the rich legacy of research and books on this topic left to us by Christian educators in the past? But the more I thought about this, the conviction began to kick in that just maybe out of those years of teaching adult Sunday School classes and the wonderful privilege of teaching Bible college students, I might be able to share some of the lessons the Lord has taught me while I endeavored to teach His people. At least, I could tell you lots of ways not to do it!

I am grateful for my family, who supported the idea of my putting these thoughts into a book, and in one of our family councils the decision was made to title it "Light Their Fire." Almost immediately my mind took me back to a quotation from John Wesley. It seems that on a certain occasion one or more of his followers came to him and asked him how they could get people to come and hear them preach. Wesley's reply was classic: "Catch on fire with enthusiasm and people will come for miles to watch you burn." Although I obviously have no way of knowing the exact meaning he was attaching to the words, "catch on fire," I believe he was referring to a Christian choosing to develop a love and passion for God, His Word, and others. If this is correct, I am intrigued by his implied analogy between this type of spiritual fire and actual physical fire. It is readily evident that the two types have at least a couple of similarities.

First, a physical fire will impact everything around it. To recognize this fact, you only need to watch some TV footage of an uncontrollable forest fire in the western part of our country as it destroys everything in its path. In a similar fashion, a Christian on fire for God is going to impact others either toward God or away from Him, if they choose to reject His truth. Second, a physical fire will attract attention. How many of us have seen in the distance a tall plume of smoke rising in the air. When informed that it is coming from a fire, we would make an effort, if possible, to get to the site to observe it firsthand. And if we manage to get to the fire, we stand almost transfixed as we watch its hungry flames consume buildings, trees, or anything else in its way. In like manner, and this is undoubtedly the point Wesley was making, if we as believers are on fire for God, many will come to check out what is taking place in our lives and ministries.

It is interesting that our Lord had a strong rebuke for those believers at Laodicea who had lost their "fire" and settled into a state of lethargy (Revelation 3:15, 16). It would seem from this passage that God's Plan A for us as Christians is that we maintain that same "first love" for Him that we experienced after our conversion. This kind of love will prioritize our agendas in such a way that our foremost concern becomes discovering and obeying His will for us each day. Sadly as we take inventory of our lives and those of other believers around us, it appears that most of us need to make some serious changes in this area.

If you are currently teaching adults in some type of Christian ministry, this is where you enter the equation. Since teaching is helping others change their behavior, and I believe we can demonstrate this later in the book, you have the potential to become a pivotal change agent for the Holy Spirit to use in igniting a fresh passion in your adults to know His truth, walk in its light, and share it with others.

If this is the longing of your heart, this book was written for you. In its pages you will find 29 "matches" or guidelines to help you "Light their fire." I apologize for the length of treatment I gave to them. While some of these "matches" were given only a few paragraphs of space, I'm afraid I was carried away with some of the others, which seem to have evolved into "mini-books" within the book. I can only trust that such shortcomings on my part will not prove to be overly distracting to the reader.

The quotations found in these pages have been collected over many years from a variety of sources: reading, conversations, broadcasts, personal reflections, etc. Since integrity demands that we give credit to the author of a quotation and repeat it accurately, research was done to track down this information. The results were a mixed bag. When names of authors were found, they were included. In some instances even the research of others has failed to identify the sources. In these situations I have simply used the words, "Author unknown." A few of these are original, born out of the Lord's dealing with me through the years. Concerning the rest, although the names of their authors may be familiar to some of you, they have eluded my search. Furthermore, given the possibility of human error in passing on these quotations, I have no guarantee that all of these statements are exact replicas of the words originally spoken or written by their authors. For those cases where I have erred in this area, I sincerely apologize. Yet the truths found in these quotations have often sparked either a smile or amen from my heart. It is my hope that they will evoke a similar response from you.

My purpose has never been to produce an exhaustive (and probably exhausting to some of you) scholarly treatise on the subject of andragogy, the art and/or science of teaching adults. It has been rather to put together a handbook with suggestions that would help sharpen the skills of those who sense God's call to teach adults, but who might not have the time to do extensive research concerning the principles and methods of adult education.

My primary target group has been some of my favorite people, that army of dedicated men and women who faithfully serve the Lord as teachers in adult Sunday school classes. Their labor of love often goes unrewarded because so few ever think to offer them a word of appreciation or encouragement. I am also hoping that this book will prove beneficial to any Christians involved in teaching adults in other types of church or church-related ministries such as teacher training programs, seminars, and home Bible studies. Since most of my teaching ministry has been in Bible colleges, much of what I have included in the book has grown out of those experiences. It would be especially gratifying to me if it were helpful to any of my co-laborers who today are seeking to train His servants in the context of formal education, ranging from a Bible institute to a Christian graduate school. If these pages prove to be of help to any of His saints, He alone deserves all the praise and glory.

Now go out there and "light their fire!"

MATCH

1

BE A CONSISTENT MODEL

He was a graduate of one of America's top evangelical seminaries. He pastored a growing Bible church. He taught Greek part-time at a nearby Bible college. He had an affair with a woman and crashed and burned, dragging down with him his ministry, his personal testimony, and the testimonies of many of his Christian friends, who were suddenly thrust into the messy role of damage control. Most of you are probably familiar with similar stories of Christian leaders, pastors, and missionaries, who fell (or probably more accurately "walked") into sin, and lost their marriages and ministries in the process. And though by the grace of God, we may not have succumbed to the same type of sins that toppled these leaders, all of us are keenly aware of our past struggles and failures while trying to live for the Lord. It is then no wonder that many Christians have been heard to say to other believers, "Don't look at my life; keep your eyes on the Lord." And while it is true that God uses terminally flawed saints (the only kind He has), it is also true that He wants us to be as holy as possible in order to model His truth before others. This is definitely a Biblical concept.

Back in the Old Testament God, in providing the perfect Model, said, "... ye shall be holy; for I am holy ..." Centuries later, God wrapped Himself in human flesh and one day stooped down to wash the dirt off His disciples' feet. Then He turned to them and said, "For I have given you an example, that ye should do as I have done to you." Most Bible believers do not interpret these words to be a mandate for establishing another ordinance for the church to observe, but rather to be a model of how we should humbly serve others. Years later, we hear the Apostle Paul repeating this theme of modeling to the early Christians. In his first letter to the Corinthians he admonishes them, "be ye followers [imitators, NASB] of me." Later, in this same letter, he urged them, "Be ye followers [same word in 4:16] of me, even as I also am of Christ." In his letter to the Philippians he encouraged them, "Brethren, be followers together of me, and mark them which walk so as ye have us for an ensample." And one chapter later, he said, "Those things, which ye have both learned, and received, and heard, and seen in me do; and the God of peace shall be with you." Ouch! I wonder how many of us as Christian teachers would be willing to say that to our classes? Then Paul seems to be passing the mantle of "modeling" on to Timothy, when he writes, "Let no man despise thy youth; but be thou an example of the believers, in word, in conversation, in charity, in spirit, in faith, in purity." From these passages, it would seem to me that the Lord is serious about Christians, living as good models of His truth which they profess to believe. This is especially critical for us as teachers, for at least two reasons.

First, if our lives contradict our lessons, our students will probably pay little, if any, attention to our lessons. Let me illustrate. You teach the men's Sunday school class. Last Sunday you were teaching from Philippians 4, and during the lesson you expounded on verse 4 and admonished your men to rejoice in the Lord always. You embellished your teaching with the use of PowerPoint and even an explanation of the passage in the original Greek text. Your lesson was indeed a thing of beauty! Then on the following Saturday, your class was playing baseball. You were at bat and managed to hit a line drive down toward the 3rd base. With all of your 195 pounds and as much wind as your 45 year- old lungs could handle, you waddled toward first base only to be greeted by a ball that arrived at the first baseman's glove approximately 3 seconds before you did and the ump's cry, "OUT!" But since you were convinced that you were faster than a speeding bullet and the ump had glaucoma, you challenged his decision. At that moment, you definitely lost it, and there at first base, you pitched your own little carnal fit. Now, which incident do you think your class members will remember: your classic S.S. lesson or your temper tantrum at first base? It really doesn't take a rocket scientist to figure out that Ralph Waldo Emerson was on target when he said, "What you do speaks so loudly I can't hear what you say." It is absolutely imperative that if we as teachers are really serious about impacting the lives of our adults for Him, we need to model the truth we seek to share with them.

Second, even if our lives exemplify our lessons, our students will remember very little of what we say in class. You may spend hours in studying and use the latest audio-visual technology in your classes, but ironically, they will not remember very many of your lessons, illustrations, jokes, etc. They will, however, remember your life. And if you have loved them, prayed for them, sought the Spirit's fullness in your ministry to them, and been a consistent model before them, THEY WILL REMEMBER THAT. Let me share with you a little experiment that I read about several years ago, and since that time, have been using in my classes. I will ask the students, "How many of you can remember five sermons you have heard that the Lord has used to impact your lives spiritually?" Then I ask them if they can, to raise their hands. Almost haltingly, three or four students will raise their hands. Then I ask them this second question, "How many of you can remember five individuals whom the Lord has used to impact your lives spiritually?" Almost immediately hands go up all over the room. My fellow teachers, I have a strong gut feeling that you will have the same experience with your students. They probably won't remember much about your lessons, but they will remember your life.

During my years of college and graduate study, I had many teachers, but in my memory, one stands out above them all. To my shame, I can't recall very much of the information he gave us in class. He was a mild-mannered introvert, who struggled with depression. In the classroom, he never raised his voice. He relied almost entirely on the lecture (not many people can get by with that), questions, and simple diagrams on the chalkboard. But even today as I sit at my computer, I can still remember this man's life. I remember his gentle smile, his reverence when he spoke about the things of God, and the love he showed toward us as his students. True, he was only a man, but he was God's man, who allowed Him to control his life and influence hundreds of college students like me, encouraging us to know Him and to make Him known. Over 50 years have passed since I graduated from that college, and I am still living in the shadow of his Godly life. It must have been this Biblical concept of modeling that caused someone years ago to pen these words: "My task as a Christian educator is not just to help you know what I know, but to BECOME WHAT I AM."

One of my favorite illustrations came from the pages of Our Daily Bread, published by the Radio Bible Class. It recounted the story of a faithful Sunday school teacher who lived years ago in Washington, D.C. It seems that he had one particular boy in his class who would not listen and continually disrupted the lesson with his misbehavior. This dedicated teacher tried everything he could to reach this boy, but nothing worked. The boy eventually grew up, left Washington, and moved out West where he proceeded to self-destruct spiritually, physically, and morally. After a number of years, for some reason, he returned to Baltimore and spent the first night there getting drunk. The next morning, trying to shake off a bad hangover, he found himself wandering the streets, finally arriving, of all places, at one of the city's cemeteries. He was shocked into sobriety when he noticed that there on one of the tombstones was the name of his former Sunday school teacher. And then, it seems as if the Holy Spirit pushed the rewind button in that man's brain, and he found himself, in his memory, listening again to many of the things his teacher had said. Pulling himself over the little railing, he went to the grave, and there, with tears, received Jesus as His Savior. After some years he entered the ministry and became the fruitful pastor of one of the most prominent churches in Virginia. That dear teacher went to his grave probably convinced that he had failed to reach that young boy in his class. But praise the Lord, even after that teacher had gone home to Glory, the godly model he left behind was used by the Spirit to bring that young man to Christ! Surely one of the many exciting things about Heaven will be to meet people who will be there, not necessarily because you had the opportunity to minister to them, but because they wanted to know for themselves the God you modeled before them. Just a closing thought for this section: you have no choice as to whether or not you will be a model. Your only choice is what kind of model you will be.

Before I leave this section, however, I need to make an additional observation. As important as it is to be a good model, that, in itself, will not guarantee that you will be an effective teacher. In fact, you can love the Lord, be a godly example, study the Word for thirty years, and even earn a Ph.D. in educational psychology, and still not be an effective teacher in the classroom.

I probably need to explain that one. Let's say that you live in Dallas, Texas, and you want to take your family to visit Washington, D.C. You have a problem, however. Your wife has a textbook case of claustrophobia, and you would have to sedate her to even get her into an airplane. So you plan to drive. Now, if you plan to arrive in Washington, together with your family and your vehicle, you will need to observe certain "laws" or "principles." At the risk of appearing severely demented, let me enumerate some of the basic ones:

1. You will need gas in your vehicle.
2. You will need enough oil in the engine.
3. You will need sufficient coolant in the engine.
4. You will need the correct air pressure in your tires.
5. You will probably need a current map with directions to Washington.
6. Finally, and this could prove to be extremely beneficial, you will need to observe the posted speed limits.

Summarily, you may have a sincere desire to drive to Washington. You may have as your objective to drive to Washington. But the simple truth is that you will not arrive in Washington unless you observe these basic principles.

My point? You may have a sincere desire to be an effective teacher. You may have as your objective to be an effective teacher, helping your adults understand God's truth and apply it to their lives. But you will not be an effective teacher unless you observe certain "laws" or "principles" pertaining to teaching. In the remaining chapters of this book, we will be looking at some of these principles and making suggestions concerning their implementation.

DEFINITELY QUOTABLE:

"If you were arrested for being a Christian, would there be enough evidence to convict you?" David Otis Fuller

"A holy minister is an awful weapon in the hand of God." Robert Murray McCheyne

STRIKE THE MATCH:

Start praying Robert McCheyne's little prayer, "Lord, make me as holy as a pardoned sinner can be."

MATCH 2

BE FILLED WITH THE SPIRIT

For years I have shared with my classes that the greatest things that have happened in my life, in order of importance, were (1) my salvation, (2) my marriage to my wonderful wife, (3) my two beautiful daughters, (4) my five precious grandchildren, (5) my computer, (6) my overhead projector, and (7) my Pomeranian dog. I think I have them in the right order! But seriously, let me talk with you for a moment about the overhead projector. Although its use has been almost eclipsed by the increasing popularity of PowerPoint, it is still a wonderful teaching tool that can make your teaching more effective. The same machine can be used to teach 5 or 5,000 (if you have a large enough screen). To get a good projector, you will probably need to spend hundreds of dollars. But if you don't have it plugged into a receptacle, where it can get power, it will never do what its maker designed it to do. And teachers, you can spend a lot of money on education, books, seminars, and high tech teaching aids. You can know Greek, Hebrew, and all the correct rules of teaching, but if you are not plugged into God's power, you will never accomplish in your classrooms what your Maker designed you to do. And when I think of God's power, I think of Acts 1:8, where Jesus promised those early believers, and us, that His Holy Spirit would give us power to witness and serve Him.

At this point, it would probably be helpful to summarize briefly what the New Testament teaches about the Holy Spirit's ministry, particularly as it relates to teaching:

1. He bestows the gift of teaching (I Corinthians 12:28).
2. He teaches, sometimes directly as in the case of Paul (Galatians 1:12) and sometimes more indirectly, through human teachers, as in the case of Apollos (Acts 18:24-26).
3. He convicts of sin (John 16:7-11).
4. He is active in the work of regeneration (Titus 3:5).
5. He is our Paraclete (John 14:16, 26). This is a beautiful word, having the idea of one who is called to walk beside us as a comforter, helper, and advocate.
6. He guides us into the truth (John 16:13).
7. He illumines, i.e., He helps us understand the meaning of the truths He has revealed in the Scriptures (Ephesians 1:17, 18).
8. He gives boldness (Acts 4:31).
9. He empowers us to win souls (Acts 11:24).

Looking over this list of the Spirit's role in the teaching process, it should seem fairly clear that if we as Christian teachers expect to make any type of lasting impact for God on our students, we desperately need to align ourselves and our teaching with the Holy Spirit and His agenda. And to my thinking, the first step in that process is to be filled, or controlled, by the Spirit. Probably the most well-known Bible verse that addresses this issue is Ephesians 5:18, where the latter part demands our special attention. Paul, under inspiration, says to us, ". . . be filled with the Spirit." While I make no claim to being a Greek scholar, I would like to share a few observations concerning these words.

1. They are in the imperative mood. This is a command. The Lord is not saying to us, "Here is a neat idea. You might want to think one day about being filled with My Spirit." No, this is His mandate for our lives and ministries.
2. The plural is used. The Lord is saying, through Paul, "All of you be filled with My Spirit." It matters not whether you are a pastor or a housewife. If you are saved, the Lord wants you to be filled with His Spirit.
3. The passive voice is used. In other words, we are to receive the filling of the Spirit.
4. And finally, but very importantly, the present tense is used. Now, for all of you who did not sleep through your high school English

classes, you will probably recall that the present tense in English generally connotes the idea of time - now. But the Greeks thought a little differently. In the language used in our New Testament, the present tense generally conveyed the idea of continuous action. So, the idea here seems to be "keep on being filled with the Spirit." This interpretation appears to be supported by the fact that the command is given to believers after the initial filling of the Spirit on the day of Pentecost (Acts 2:4) and a subsequent filling following an outbreak of opposition from the Jews (Acts 4:31).

At this point, a story I heard many years ago seems appropriate. It seemed that in this particular church, there was this one man who was living a lifestyle definitely not very Christlike. But he would come to church and during prayer time, would say, "O Lord, fill me, fill me." Well, this pattern of living a backslidden life during the week and praying for the Lord to fill him went on for some time. Finally, there was one saint in the church who grew tired of this man's hypocrisy, and so on one occasion when he was praying his favorite prayer "O Lord, fill me," this saint cried out so all could hear him, "DON'T DO IT, LORD. HE LEAKS!" And you know, he was right. In fact, because of our sins and failures, we all leak spiritually. You may have been Spirit-filled the last time you taught a group of adults, and the Lord blessed and used your lesson to work in their lives, but that spiritual victory won't carry you through the next time you teach. We definitely need to be filled with the Spirit continually. In fact, summarizing the preceding observations, it might be appropriate to paraphrase the latter half of Ephesians 5:18 this way: "ALL OF YOU KEEP ON BEING FILLED WITH THE HOLY SPIRIT."

The question as to how we may be filled with the Spirit might possibly be clarified if we could think of being filled with Him as being controlled by Him. This seems to be the point Paul is trying to make in Ephesians 5:18. Look at it again. "And be not drunk with wine, wherein is excess [when a person is drunk, the wine takes control and affects his actions and words]; but be filled with the Spirit" In a parallel fashion, when the Spirit of God fills us, He takes control of us and affects our actions, words, and ministry. Personally, I am convinced that there are at least two prerequisites we must meet, if we are to be filled or controlled by the Spirit.

First, we need to keep our sins confessed. This confession should be first of all to God and then to others if necessary and appropriate. As most of us have found out the hard way, unconfessed sins in our lives will short-circuit the power of God in our ministries. Sometimes I think the devil has a special group of demons, whom he perhaps calls his "Sunday Specialty Squad." Their primary mission is to invade the homes of Christians, especially teachers and pastors, on Sunday mornings between the hours of 7:00 and 9:00 a.m. and get family members fighting and fussing over incredibly strategic issues, such as who burned the toast or who was supposed to walk the dog after breakfast. As a result, we yell and/or pout all the way to the church parking lot, at which point we reach into the glove compartment and pull out our "Sunday face," which bears a strong resemblance to Michael the archangel. But though we fool the other Christians in the vestibule and class, when we stand up to teach, we find to our dismay that the Spirit of God "remains seated" and will have no part in our masquerade, consequently withholding His hand of blessing from our teaching. Results? We end up winging it in the flesh and accomplishing precious little that will last into eternity. Sound familiar? The solution? Keep short accounts with God. When I sin, I need to claim I John 1:9 and confess it to God at once. If I have sinned against another, e.g., lost my temper, spoken unkindly to my wife and hurt her, I need to confess that to God and then to her ASAP. By the way, a good rule of thumb concerning confessing sins is that the confession should only be as public as the sin. If you have a big argument with your wife on Saturday night and she runs home to her mother's overnight, it is probably not necessary to share that little tidbit with your entire class on Sunday morning. The bottom line to this paragraph is a statement I heard years ago that the Lord burned into my mind: "God does not demand a beautiful vessel, but He does demand a clean one."

   A second prerequisite for being filled with the Spirit is to allow Jesus complete control of your life. One of the best illustrations I have ever heard concerning this truth was given by the late Oswald Smith, who served as pastor years ago of the great People's Church in Toronto. The details of this story have grown fuzzy, so I will just give you the gist of it. Let's say that I sell you my house. After all the work at the bank, inspection of the house, signing of papers, etc., I give you the keys, and you move into your new home. You move in your furniture and get it all decorated just the way you and your family like it. After a few months, you come home one day and find the door to one of the bedrooms locked.

None of your keys work, and you don't want to break down the door. So you end up calling me and explaining your plight. To which, I say, "O, sorry about that. You see, I needed a place to store some of my stuff, so I came over the other day while you were gone, put my things in, changed the lock, and came on home." Well, you get just a little upset. In fact, you get downright hostile. You then proceed to remind me in no uncertain terms that you bought that house, the mortgage is in your name, and if I don't get over there pronto and get my stuff out of your house, I can expect a visit very soon from the guys in blue.

Now I realize this scenario is totally ridiculous, but isn't this exactly how we treat the Lord? Jesus left Heaven and came down here to suffer one of the most horrible deaths that men have been able to imagine. Why? Because He loved us, and when He died on that cross, He paid with His blood to redeem us from sin and hell and to make us a temple for His Holy Spirit. Just as an aside, I personally think He paid too much for what He received for that payment, but I will be eternally glad that He did. Amen. To paraphrase this awesome truth, Jesus bought you and me as a house in which He may live. Amazing! Someone put it this way, "One of the mysteries of the ages is that the eternal Creator would choose to live in clay pots that He made." But back to Smith's illustration. When we get saved, I believe we hand all the keys over to the Lord. His Spirit moves into our lives, occupying "all the rooms" and initially producing those wonderful fruits listed in Galatians 5. But over the course of the days, as all of us are painfully aware, we tend "to lock the Lord out of some of the rooms in our hearts." It may be the problem of a besetting sin. So, we tell the Lord, "You can have all of my heart, but this little area right here, this little sin, I want to hang on to." Or it may be the problem of an unforgiving spirit. "Lord, I just can't forgive and forget the way he talked to me last week." Results? The omnipotent Spirit of God is grieved, quenched, and will not share with us His power in our ministry. The solution? Come to the Lord in genuine repentance and confession and "give Him back all the keys to our heart." In this day when Christians seem to be fascinated by the potential of high tech methodology, it might be good to remember that the Holy Spirit of God does not fill nor use methods (laptop, multimedia projectors, etc.). He fills and uses men and women who are yielded completely to Him.

When we sincerely meet these two prerequisites, confessing our known sins and making ourselves unconditionally available to the Holy Spirit's control, I believe He will fill us. And while I doubt seriously that we will see any celestial fireworks or visions, I am convinced we shall see Him make a difference in our lives and ministries. In the New Testament, it is interesting to note some of the consequences of those believers being filled with the Spirit:

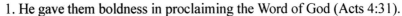

1. He gave them boldness in proclaiming the Word of God (Acts 4:31).
2. He used them to win souls (Acts 11:24).
3. He produced in them His fruit (Galatians 5:22, 23).
4. He produced in them a spirit of worship (Ephesians 5:18-20).

After reading over these passages, I feel a little like that old preacher, who, reflecting on some of God's gracious visitations of revival in the past, prayed, "O Lord, do it again!" Teachers, I hope that is also the prayer of your heart right now.

DEFINITELY QUOTABLE:

"The Holy Ghost does not flow through methods, but through men. He does not come on machinery, but on men. He does not anoint plans, but men - men of prayer." E. M. Bounds

STRIKE THE MATCH:

Each time you have the opportunity to teach a group of adults, try to set aside some time beforehand to get alone with the Lord. Ask Him to search your heart and show you any sins that might be blocking the flow of His power in your life. Confess each of those sins to Him, and if possible before you begin teaching, make things right with anyone else you may have offended. Then by faith, give Him "all the keys to your heart" and ask the Holy Spirit to take control again of your life and use you for His glory.

MATCH

3

PRAY! PRAY! PRAY!

When I mention the word teaching, what is the first thing that comes to your mind? For some of you, it will be a classroom, with rows of chairs, some type of lectern, a teacher, and some students. And while those ingredients will probably be present in most classes in formal education, if you are a teacher, seeking to share God's truth with others, there is something far more serious going on "behind the scenes." Christian teacher, every time you stand up to teach those adults, a spiritual battle will be raging as the Spirit of God wars with the devil for the hearts and wills of the men and women in your class. And while you will need to use sound principles and methods of teaching, you will never be successful in this area of spiritual warfare, unless you learn to use the correct type of spiritual weapons. Failing to do so could be compared to sending an elite group of Army Rangers, armed with slingshots into battle today. Paul was keenly aware of the true nature of our conflict when he wrote, "For we wrestle not against flesh and blood, but against principalities, against powers, against the rulers of the darkness of this world, against spiritual wickedness in high places" (Ephesians 6:12). But God has provided us with the kind of weapons needed to get the job done, as the Apostle in II Corinthians 10:4 reminded us, "For the weapons of our warfare are not carnal [of the flesh, NASB], but mighty through God to the pulling down of strong holds." Then he proceeded to enumerate those types of weapons in that familiar passage in Ephesians 6:16-18, where he concluded his list with this admonition, "Praying always with all prayer and supplication in the Spirit, and watching thereunto with all perseverance and supplication for all saints." Time will only permit us briefly to pick up and examine this weapon of prayer.

I am keenly aware of the fact that many believers have disagreed and will probably continue to disagree with what I'm about to say, but I feel I must share this conviction with you. It seems to me that it is not just a question of prayer being a vital weapon in our spiritual battles, but in God's economy, there seems to be a direct correlation between time spent in prayer and the measure of His power we experience in our ministry. I still remember those college years, when I would hear our godly president, Dr. Robert McQuilken, often remind us of this truth with the simple, little equation: "Little prayer - little blessing; more prayer - more blessing; much prayer - much blessing." Now, don't misunderstand me. I don't see God in heaven with a stopwatch, watching us pray and saying, "O.K., My child, you are doing great. Just hang in there for one more hour of prayer, and I am really going to bless you!" Yet, when we look at church history, it seems evident that some of the spiritual giants whom God used mightily were individuals who were committed to spending sizable blocks of time in intercessory prayer.

This principle was clearly demonstrated years ago in the periodical <u>Herald of His Coming</u> where one of its articles recorded the following illustrations: (1) Martin Luther might spend three hours a day in prayer; (2) John Knox would spend nights in prayer, crying out to God for his beloved Scotland; (3) John Wesley in his journals, told of entire nights of intercession for the ministry there in England; and (4) David Brainerd, suffering with tuberculosis, used to lie on the frozen ground at night, wrapped in a bear's skin, and cry out to the Lord to save the American Indians. Then there was Jonathan Edwards who was known to spend fifteen to sixteen hours a day in Bible study and prayer. I have a strong suspicion that there was a distinct correlation between Edwards' prayer life and the power of God unleashed when he preached his famous sermon, "Sinners in the Hands of an Angry God." And certainly no catalog of prayer warriors in the church would be complete without mentioning George Mueller. This great hero of faith was used of God to pray in the funds necessary to feed and house thousands of orphans in England and also to support missionary work throughout the world. In his biography <u>George Mueller: Man of Faith</u> we learn that he would get alone with his Bible and pray for hours.

My personal response to the accomplishments of these prayer giants is mixed. The Spirit of God within agrees that this is His Plan A. But I have a major problem. My old nature wants to resist, and frankly I struggle with this matter of spending extended times with the Lord in prayer. I confess that I am a "Jacob" who wants to make things happen with my little plans, organizational charts, and job descriptions. I tend to make my personal plan B, hold it up to God and ask Him to "sign off on it" rather than spend time before Him, give Him a "blank piece of paper," and ask Him to fill in the details of His perfect plan. I struggle with drowsiness, especially if I kneel to pray. I have problems with my mind wandering. At times I will be having my quiet time with the Lord in the morning, and during my prayer time, I will notice that a picture is hanging crooked on the wall. So, what do I do? I walk across the room and straighten the picture! Ridiculous! Then there are those times praying, when I feel as if I am talking "to the wall." Does any of this sound a bit familiar to some of you? I have a hunch that it does. Let me make a few suggestions that have been helpful not only to me, but also to many of God's people.

1. If possible, try walking while you are praying. At least this will make it a bit more difficult to fall asleep. Not impossible, just difficult. My wife once worked with a woman who could go to sleep standing at her job!
2. If possible, and it won't disturb others, pray aloud, or at least, form the words with your lips.
3. If possible, look into the heavens, trying to picture the Father listening to you.
4. Ask the Spirit, Who produces the fruit of self-control, to help you discipline yourself to spend that necessary time with the Father.
5. Make a prayer list. Use it daily, but be careful that it doesn't become just an "evangelical rosary" that you repeat mechanically every day and forget you are talking to your Father. For ideas on how you might want to organize your prayer list, see the sample in Appendix A.

And though, as I mentioned earlier, my flesh resists spending extended seasons of prayer with the Lord, when I have been willing to pay the price of giving myself to Him in that kind of praying, He has come in blessing. During some of these prayer times, He will seem so real and precious, you can almost reach out and touch Him. You may even be able to relate to that believer, who after sensing the awesome presence of God while praying, exclaimed that he felt "like God had busted a keg of honey in his soul!" But regardless of how this type of praying affects your feelings, it will surely affect your ministry, producing results that only His presence and power can explain.

DEFINITELY QUOTABLE:

"The men who have done the most for God in this world have been early on their knees." E.M. Bounds

"I will be so busy today that I cannot have less than two hours for prayer." John Wesley

STRIKE THE MATCH:

If you have not done so already, make a covenant with the Lord that you will set aside some time each day to meet Him in the Word and prayer. Mornings seem to work best for many Christians, but you may not be a "morning person," so pick the time when you will feel the most alert and focused. During the week some of the "must" items to bring before Him include the following: the names and needs of the individuals whom you teach; His wisdom and guidance in preparing just the message He wants them to hear; and His power to communicate that message in such a way that when you finish your lesson, your adults will love Him more and want to serve Him.

MATCH

4

LOVE YOUR ADULTS AND DEMONSTRATE IT

What is love? The following comments of kids on this subject have been circulating the internet for years, so there is no way I am going to vouch for their accuracy. But let's face it; they do make a great introduction to this chapter!

"I'm in favor of love as long as it doesn't happen when The Simpsons is on television."   Anita, 6

"Love will find you, even if you are trying to hide from it. I have been trying to hide from it since I was five, but the girls keep finding me." Bobby, 8

"I'm not rushing into being in love. I'm finding fourth grade hard enough." Regina, 10

"I think you're supposed to get shot with an arrow or something, but the rest of it isn't supposed to be so painful." Harlan, 8

On a darker side, we live in a day when the American media and music industries have so prostituted the concept of love that it often carries little more significance than lust, depicting the efforts of one individual to use others in order to gratify self. This type of thinking is light years away from God's meaning of the word "loved" found in John 3:16. This word has been translated from the Greek word agape and could be defined as purposing the welfare of others even above that of your own.

Surely this beloved verse becomes prophetic of Calvary, where we see that God loved us and purposed our welfare even above the welfare of His own precious Son, to the extent that He was willing to let Him suffer one of the most horrible deaths known in history, in order to redeem us and bring us into His family. We did not love Him, as the Apostle John reminds us in I John 4, but He loved us. Tremendous display of genuine love! Now, God turns to us as His redeemed children and commands us to demonstrate that same kind of love to others.

At this point, it might be profitable to digress just a bit and look at two verses in the fifth chapter of Ephesians, where Paul uses that same Greek word in his two analogies to explain the relationship that husbands should have with their wives. In verse 25, husbands are commanded to love their wives as Christ loved the Church. And in 5:28, husbands are commanded to love their wives just as they love their own bodies. It is interesting that liberals don't have much to say about these verses, but they can go into a "feeding frenzy" over Paul's admonition in 5:22 for wives to be in submission to their husbands. One of them, Okot p'Bitek, even accused Paul of being "a great woman hater." But again these same liberals seem to conveniently forget verse 25. My reply to them is, if a man loves his wife with any amount of devotion that approximates the agape love Christ has for His Church, that wife would be a fool not to submit to him, for he would have only her best interests at heart.

But let me get back to the purpose for including this Match. Surely our Lord's command to love our fellow believers will also apply to our relationship to the men and women whom we teach. And just as God's love toward us was demonstrated at Calvary and in all the many blessings He has poured into our lives, we need to demonstrate to our adults that we love them. Let me suggest a number of ways which might be particularly helpful to those of you who teach adult Sunday School classes.

1. Pray for them regularly. Some time ago, I was talking to one of the finest young men in our church, and he asked me, "How can I pray for you?" Knowing that man as I do, I feel this was a request born out of a genuine concern for me, and it touched me very much that he cared. If you use a prayer list (a sample is shown in Appendix A), put the names of all your class members on your list, and at least

weekly, pray through those names. Some teachers of adults, before they begin their lesson, will ask the class for prayer requests. Unfortunately, in many cases, we end up taking about 10-12 requests, call on someone to lead the class in prayer, and that person never even mentions one of the requests, but prays such a generic prayer, that we would not recognize the answer if the Lord sent it! If you are in the custom of asking for prayer requests before your lesson, here are some suggestions to consider.

  a. Select an adult to list on a board the prayer requests as they are mentioned.
  b. Call on one adult to pray for as many of the requests as can be remembered, or simply go down the list of requests and for each one, ask a volunteer to pray briefly and specifically for that one request later during your prayer session.
  c. Give a 3x5 card to each adult present and ask each to use that card to print their name and a specific prayer request. Collect those cards and mix them up in a bowl or offering plate. Ask each adult to take one of them and pray for that individual and the request each day of the coming week.

One final point. If one of your class members asks you to pray for a certain need, and you agree to do so, as soon as you leave that person, send a S.O.S. up to Heaven for that request. Sadly, in too many instances, we are sincere in our promise to pray for a person, but we walk away and forget to do so.

2. Be a friend to every member of the class. If you are married, this must also apply to your spouse. Due to similarities in education, personalities, or level of spiritual maturity, it is almost inevitable that you will "click" with some of your members more than others. But if this attraction leads you to select such individuals as your favorite golfing or fishing buddies, it probably will not take very long for some heavy-duty resentment to surface, thereby limiting your effectiveness in ministering to the entire group.

3. Be an encourager. When, not if (!), we see our class members experiencing trials, such as sickness, financial emergencies, problems with their children, death of a loved one, etc., don't just say, "If there is anything I can do for you, just let me know." Sadly, in too many cases, this is just another example of "Christian speak" which is hypoc-

risy at its worst, and unfulfilled intentions at its best. No, be there for them! Let your loving support in those times be incarnated in a word of encouragement, a hug, tears of sympathy, a phone call, a written message, a visit to the home with a meal, a bouquet of flowers, or any number of ways, limited only by your lack of concern or creativity.

4. Remember their birthdays. Unless you teach senior adults, ages 75 and above, I recommend that you cool the idea of cake and candles. But cards are always appropriate. Either purchase them or design your own with your computer. THE important point here is that if you start this practice of sending cards to your class members, and I think that it is a great idea, just don't forget anyone! As some of you may know, there is computer software that will flag you with a reminder of upcoming, important birthdays. If you are not that computer "savvy," you will need to work out some idiot-proof plan that will ensure your sending a card to each member before the actual birthday.

Years ago I had the privilege of teaching a young married couples class for about a year and found this idea helpful. I bought a supply of 3x5 cards and used one card for each member of the class. On the left side of the card I printed that member's name, address, phone number. In the upper right hand corner I printed the member's birthday, e.g. September 9. After filling out a card for each member, I arranged all the cards in the order of their birthdays, from January to December, put a rubber band around them, and placed them inside my Bible in the spot where I was having my daily Bible reading. That way, each morning as I opened my Bible, I could see whose birthday was coming up next. After addressing a birthday card to that individual, I would place their "date" card on the bottom of the stack and wait for the next birthday. This is obviously a no-brainer, but it worked for me (which probably makes a statement concerning my IQ level).

5. Get to your classroom early. When you get all your stuff ready to teach, spend the rest of the time before class starts just moving among your members, shaking hands, exchanging news, asking about their health, etc. One veteran Sunday School teacher even suggested that if you can get to your room before anyone else arrives and can remember where your class members usually sit, walk around the room and as you look at the chairs, pray for those who will be sitting in them.

6. Be sure to extend a genuinely warm welcome to each visitor and follow up that visit with a card, phone call, or visit to the person's home. And here's a couple of ideas spinning off this. See if you can enlist a couple of spiritual, outgoing class members to be designated "Greeters" (some church growth gurus have recommended that you refer to such a person as a "Host" or Hostess") to welcome these visitors each week. And when you as the teacher send the visitors a written message, be sure it is just that. Write it out by hand. Of course if your handwriting is as bad as mine and strongly resembles some form of Egyptian hieroglyphics, you may want to enlist someone else to write the note. I don't recommend any type of computer-generated memo, because it seems to come across as definitely less personal.

7. Learn all their names. In a small church, this will probably be no big deal, but in a larger class, you could have between 20-100 members. It is absolutely imperative that you try to learn their names as soon as possible. I have included some ideas with Match # 8. As an aside, years ago a prominent Christian educator stated that he felt a class was too large if the teacher did not know every student. But regardless of the size of your class, you need to keep in mind that the person to whom you are speaking may have a thousand friends who call his/her name, but if you want to demonstrate your love and friendship toward individuals, you need to know and use their names. This is not an inspired mandate for you, just food for thought.

8. When they are talking to you, look them in the eyes and listen attentively. Try not to start formulating a reply until they have finished speaking. God in His infinite wisdom gave us only one mouth but two ears. I think He may have been trying to tell us something.

9. Keep their confidences, when they share their deep seated concerns with you. Don't violate their trust by sharing this information with others or using them as illustrations in future lessons.

10. Never carry gossip and/or criticism of one member to another one. Gossip has been termed "the favorite indoor sport of Christians." Unfortunately, we have learned how to mask gossip by "baptizing it" with the spiritual sounding introduction, "This is something we really need to pray about." This mentality reminds me of the statement, "The Christian army is the only army in the world that shoots

its wounded in the back."

11. If you can accommodate the entire class, open your home for special events (for example, a Christmas party). I read recently about a teacher who would launch her hospitality venture with each new class by inviting them to her home for a chili supper.

12. Maintain contact with faithful members who can no longer attend your class because of their illness or their role as a care giver for a loved one. Here's an idea you might want to try in such cases. Years ago, one of the couples in our Sunday school class had to drop out because of the husband's sickness. So we decided if they could not come to class, we would take the class to them. We made arrangements to videotape a lesson, and at the end of the class, taped various members giving a personal greeting to the couple, assuring them of our loving concern and prayers. Later, the wife tearfully shared with us that this tape had meant so much to them, that they had played it repeatedly during the following days.

13. Finally, keep in mind that your love for them may also, at times, include hurting them. As an illustration, let's say that you develop a medical condition that threatens to take your life, unless you have surgery. On the day of your surgery, the doctor comes to your door and with an aerosol can, sprays some antiseptic in the room, and tells you that this will heal you. Absurd! Humanly speaking, the only thing that is going to save your life is the scalpel in the hands of a skilled surgeon. In a similar fashion, there will come those times if you really love your class, you will need to hurt or rebuke them. This should always be accompanied, however, with the extended promise of God's forgiveness and grace to move on for Him.

This list is definitely not exhaustive, but intended only to "prime your pump." Your genuine love for your class, coupled with a bit of creativity, will certainly produce many other ways to express itself for them.

DEFINITELY QUOTABLE:

"I expect to pass through this world but once; any good thing therefore that I can do or any kindness that I can show to any fellow creature,

let me do it now; let me not defer or neglect it, for I shall not pass this way again." Stephen Grellet

"Kindness is the language which the deaf can hear and the blind can see." Mark Twain

"To love the whole world for me is no chore; my only real problem's my neighbor next door." C. W. Vanderburgh

STRIKE THE MATCH:

If you are a teacher of an adult Sunday school class try to review the suggestions in this section before next Sunday and if possible seek to implement one or two of them with your adults. For example, if you do not yet have some type of workable plan for remembering the birthdays of your members, determine if any of the ideas shared here will work for you. Putting some type of plan into action ASAP will serve as an additional means to demonstrate your love and concern for your class.

MATCH

5

KEEP YOURSELF AS PHYSICALLY ATTRACTIVE AS POSSIBLE

We Americans seem to have a love affair with this thing called youth and good looks in our culture today. Unfortunately, the passing of time does not treat either of these items with much kindness. In fact, just try this little experiment. Go out to a place, frequented by large crowds of people, such as a shopping mall. Take a seat and just observe the people who pass by. It won't take you very long to come to the conclusion that at least by Hollywood's standards, there aren't very many handsome men nor beautiful women. Most of us look, well . . . sort of average. But if people are going to have to look at us while we are teaching them, we ought to do what we can to make ourselves as easy to look at as possible. Or as one preacher put it so aptly, "If the barn needs painting, paint it!"

Here's a suggestion. Before you teach your adults, find a mirror and
go through this checklist:

1. Did you brush your teeth? No one really enjoys seeing the remnants of your last meal firmly embedded between two of your front teeth.
2. If you are a man and wearing a tie, is its knot correctly in place, and more importantly, is it clean? If it is still decorated with last Sunday's gravy, the time has probably arrived to have it cleaned or trashed.
3. And men, this one is also for you. Be sure that your nose and ear hairs are clipped. They may add something to your facial landscape, but they really don't add a whole lot to your lesson!

4. Is your hair neatly combed or brushed? If you are balding like me, you probably don't comb it; you just try to arrange it neatly.
5. Are there any stains on your clothes? You may be teaching a group of adults, and Joe on the front row seems absolutely mesmerized as he gazes at you intently while you teach. But before you start congratulating yourself on your extraordinary pedagogical skills, keep in mind that he may only be staring at the bloody spot on your collar, left there because you cut yourself shaving that morning.

6. Do you have a supply of breath fresheners to place in your mouth before you walk into your room and especially after you finish your lesson? There is something about teaching or preaching that may give you a nasty case of "dragon breath." Also, be careful about drinking coffee before or during your teaching. It has been known to create a "killing field" up to a foot in front of you!

DEFINITELY QUOTABLE:

"*Time may be a great healer, but it's a lousy beautician.*" *Author unknown*

"*A real friend will tell you when you have spinach stuck in your teeth.*" E.C. McKenzie

STRIKE THE MATCH:

Before you teach next time, find a mirror and ask yourself the questions listed above. If you can't get to a mirror, I'm reasonably sure you must have some friend who will be glad to furnish you the answers.

MATCH

6

BE SURE YOU ARE TEACHING - NOT JUST TALKING

Undoubtedly, the name of this Match has some of you scratching your head and questioning my sanity. Cheer up and welcome to the club. My wife has been wondering about that for years! But hopefully, its wording did get your attention. I fully realize that many Christian teachers define teaching as primarily the process of transmitting information to others, and therefore, the method most commonly used is talking or lecturing.

I would like to suggest another definition, which initially may sound rather radical. I believe that while teaching many times does indeed involve talking, there is something else going on in the process. Let me illustrate. If I were to tell you one day that I had taught my daughter how to ride a bicycle, what would you obviously conclude? That she had learned how to ride her bicycle. There had been a change in her behavior.

Following that logic, let me suggest an alternate definition of teaching. It is the process of helping individuals change their behavior in one or more of the following areas:

1. Concepts. As a result of your teaching, your adults have learned definitions of terms, the meaning of a certain Biblical passage, how to interpret parables, etc.
2. Attitudes and/or values (which generally drive our behavior). As a result of your teaching, your class members followed the Biblical ethic of honesty when filling out their income tax forms.

3. Physical skills. As a result of your teaching a first aid class in your church, a member learns how to administer the Heimlich Maneuver and is later able at a picnic to save a friend from choking to death.

If teaching is indeed helping individuals change their behavior, and after many years at this job, I am more than ever convinced it is, then I'm afraid that much of what we have been calling teaching in Christian education is in reality not much more than just talking. In fact, I believe it is possible for us to talk for an hour and teach little, if anything. Then how will we know if we have actually been teaching? If we accept the definition of teaching as the process of helping individuals change their behavior, the answer to that question should eventually be evident. Has there been any change in the behavior of your adults in their understanding, attitudes/values, and skills? But just a word of caution, lest you get discouraged as you look, sometimes in vain, for changes especially in the area of spiritual maturity in individuals. We have instant potatoes and instant oatmeal, but we don't have any instant saints! And while it is true that at the instant of conversion we positionally become saints (set apart in Christ), the process of growing a saint into the likeness of Christ takes time. Lots of time. If you have any doubts about that statement, think about what your life was like before Jesus saved you. Then think about how long it has taken you to reach your level of spiritual maturity (assuming, of course there has been some maturing). Now take a really good look at Jesus, in Whose likeness the Spirit is seeking to form us (Romans 8:29), and I think you will find yourself agreeing with the Apostle Paul, "Not as though I had already attained . . ." (Philippians 3:12).

O.K., so you buy this definition. Now, the big problem is how do you make this all happen and teach in such a way that it will result in changed behavior in your adults? We will seek to address this question with some of the other matches in the book.

DEFINITELY QUOTABLE:

"Teaching is not talking, and listening is not learning." Debbie Meier
"The teacher has not taught until the learner has learned." Henrietta Mears

STRIKE THE MATCH:

Begin praying that the Lord will keep you as a teacher from being merely a transmitter of Biblical data, but will use you as a genuine change agent as He seeks to mold your adults into the image of His Dear Son.

MATCH

7

REMEMBER WHOM YOU ARE TEACHING

Someone once said, "You are not teaching lessons; you are teaching people." I agree, and therefore, it is my conviction that the more you know about the adults you are teaching, i.e., their characteristics, needs, and problems, the more effective you will be as a teacher in ministering to them. Our initial problem, however, is knowing what to call them. This is complicated by the fact that the media gurus keep changing the politically correct landscape, as they assign to different groups such names as Baby Boomers, Baby Busters, Generation X'ers., and Twixters. So rather than fight that losing battle, I have preferred to resort to the designations used by Christian educators for years: young adults (ages 18-34), middle-aged adults (ages 35-64), and senior adults (ages 65+). The following profiles of these categories are very general. The operative word in that statement is surely "general." These lists are far from exhaustive, and as you consider the particular group of adults you are teaching, you will probably be able to add a number of other characteristics to that list. Incidentally, the traits shown below are not arranged in any order of importance.

A GENERAL PROFILE OF YOUNG ADULTS (AGES 18-34)

1. They are concerned/worried about economic issues such as finding a good job following high school graduation and later keeping a job as a thirty year old, young married man, with two children and a thirty year mortgage.

2. After being stung by the moral collapse of so many "respected leaders," such as politicians, pastors, evangelists, and missionaries, these adults tend to be somewhat cynical about those in authority. This thinking was probably best captured in the wording on a bumper sticker I saw recently. It said simply, "Question authority."
3. Those entering the first years of this period face some of the most critical decisions of their lives. The most important one is what they will do with Jesus: accept Him as Savior or go their own way, ignoring His gracious offer of salvation. Some will need to choose a college, and possibly consider graduate work after that. Many will be selecting a marriage partner and seeking to build a successful marriage, including rearing children and handling a mortgage. Eventually, all will be looking for a vocation or a ministry. Incidentally, it is not uncommon to hear of individuals who are earning top dollars in their jobs, but finding themselves bored and unfulfilled.
4. For those who move through this period still unmarried, there is the problem of controlling a God-given sex drive while living in a sex-obsessed culture.
5. Many of them have been hypnotized by materialism and the "good life" with its nice homes, cars, and all those expensive "toys," which are so readily available with a piece of plastic.
6. They tend to accept the postmodern concept of truth, which asserts that truth and ethics are not objective nor absolute, but rather subjective and relative, simply a matter of individual choice. If you need any proof of how deeply postmodernity has affected America's concept of absolutes in truth, simply declare your conviction that Jesus Christ is the only way to Heaven (John 14:6) and watch the firestorm that statement will create. If you want evidence of how postmodernity has affected our country's concept of absolutes in ethics, share your conviction that homosexuality is not a condition, such as being left-handed, but actually a sinful lifestyle, that God will judge. If you have watched any talk shows recently on TV, you have seen the world's reaction to that one! Obviously, if you are a Sunday school teacher in an evangelical church, you may not encounter much of this type of thinking (can't guarantee that one), but as your church reaches out to witness to the unsaved and bring them under its influence, you should be prepared to deal with postmodernity.
7. They are very visually oriented. Many of them spend hours each week viewing digitally enhanced films, watching color monitors

(often surpassing the quality of color in 35 mm film), and working with laptop computers. Consequently don't expect them to sit in rapt attention in your class, while you lecture in a monotone for 45 minutes on the return of Ezra to Jerusalem.
8. Many of them have a problem making commitments "for the long haul." This is reflected in the alarming divorce rate among Christian couples, and also in their hesitancy in getting involved in the ministry of the local church.

A GENERAL PROFILE OF MIDDLE AGED ADULTS (AGES 35-64)

Someone has defined middle age as "that time of life when your age starts to show up around your middle." It has been given many other interesting titles, but my favorite is "the time of Bulges, Baldness, Bunions, Bifocals, Boomerang kids (those who move out of the home for some reason but later return), and Batteries (for hearing aids)." Again, the following description of middle age is both generic and brief, but if you work with this age group, hopefully the list will enable you to understand them a bit better.

1. Later in this period there is a gradual decrease in strength and energy. This may be especially dangerous for men, who at age 53 think they can still go out on the tennis court and play like they did at age 20.
2. Many will tend to gain weight, either due to lack of exercise or taking certain medications. Commenting on this fact, someone facetiously made this observation: "Middle age is that period when a narrow waist and a broad mind swap places."
3. Their hair turns gray or "turns loose."
4. Their vision and hearing will become impaired. This time of life brings an introduction into the wonderful world of bifocals or trifocals, and the sudden appearance of ridiculously small print in Bibles, newspapers, and the directions on medicine bottles.
5. As they move on through this time period, they are introduced to a whole new host of exciting diseases and illnesses, such as arthritis, diverticulosis, and kidney stones. Many times when I hear of kidney stones, I am reminded of the fellow who said, after passing a kidney stone, that he had given birth to a pet rock!
6. Their capacity to learn remains virtually unchanged until old age, but as they grow older, they will experience a gradual decline in the rate of learning.
7. Toward the end of this period, many of them tend to resist change or

anything that may threaten to move them out of their "comfort zone."
8. Rearing the children, in some cases, becomes problematic, especially when those children become teenagers and rebel against the Christian truths and values they have been taught.
9. Sometimes paying for the college education of children adds financial stress.
10. Some experience problems adjusting to the departure of the children from the home. For some mothers who have lived at home with the children, their leaving can trigger the onset of boredom and/or depression. For others, whose marriage has been kept together because of their mutual interaction with their children, the loss of that "glue" often causes the marriage to unravel and propels them to the divorce court.
11. For some husbands, who lose their jobs late in this period, finding new employment can be very stressful. In one case I know about, a Christian man who lost his job late in life could not handle this crisis, and eventually committed suicide.
12. Some will lose their mate, perhaps through a painful, protracted illness, such as cancer. Irrespective of the circumstances of the death, someone has aptly referred to the loss of one's mate as a "psychological amputation."
13. Many of them eventually will face the problem of how to care for aging parents, who no longer are able to live by themselves.
14. Many will experience trouble in their marriages that results in separation and divorce, with all the problems related to that painful experience, such as the wife rearing the children alone while struggling to meet financial needs.
15. For those who never marry, there are problems related to remaining single, such as loneliness, frustration over their childlessness, and having their sexual orientation questioned by others.
16. Most of them, sometime during this period, will experience what has been termed a "mid-life crisis." Defining this term is difficult. For some, the aging process becomes a bit traumatic, and they will do almost anything to give the appearance of reversing this process. Some women will fight back with injections of Botox or procedures such as liposuction. Some men may leave open the top two buttons of their shirts to show off their chest hairs, buy a gold necklace, squeeze into a pair of jeans, two sizes too small, or go out and buy a new sports car. For many Christians, growing older becomes a spiri-

tual "wake-up call" that causes them to reorder their priorities as they realize they have so little time left and will soon see Jesus to give account to Him for what they have done with their lives.

A GENERAL PROFILE OF SENIOR ADULTS (AGES 65 -)

Many of you reading this section are acquainted with this age group primarily through your relationships with your parents or grandparents. But if our Lord tarries His coming, and you live long enough, you will get to know experientially many of the following characteristics of senior adults.

1. Their level of strength and energy is declining, and they become fatigued more easily.
2. Many of them will suffer with those chronic diseases frequently associated with the aging process, such as arthritis, bursitis, diabetes, hypertension, heart problems, and dementia (an umbrella term for those conditions such as Alzheimer's disease and Atherosclerosis)
3. Problems, such as cataracts and Glaucoma, cause a decline in vision. Because night driving for many will become more difficult, churches with senior ministries schedule most of those activities during the daylight hours.
4. By the age of forty, a noticeable decline in hearing can sometimes be detected, but it usually does not become much of a problem until late adulthood. At that time some hearing difficulties may need to be corrected with hearing aids.
5. Their bones become more brittle, break more easily, and heal more slowly. I recently heard of some senior age women who were willing to come to Sunday school, but afraid to stay for the morning worship service, for fear of being jostled in the crowd and falling.
6. As people grow older, they get shorter. Their bodies cannot continue to resist gravity, and as their muscles weaken, their backs may begin to slump.
7. They can still learn, but it may take them a little longer.
8. Jokes about seniors' memory problems are legion, and here is one of my favorite poems.

"A Little Mixed Up"

Just a line to say I'm living,
That I'm not among the dead.
Though I'm getting more forgetful

And mixed up in my head.

*I've got used to my arthritis,
To my dentures I'm resigned.
I can manage my bifocals,
But, oh my! I miss my mind.*

*For sometimes I can't remember
When I stand at the foot of the stairs,
If I must go up for something
Or, I've just come down from there.*

*And, before the refrigerator so often,
My poor mind is filled with doubt.
Have I just put food away, or
Have I come to take some out?*

*And there's times when it is dark,
With my night cap on my head
I don't know if I'm retiring,
Or just got out of bed.*

*So, if it's my turn to write you,
There's no need of getting sore.
I may think that I have written,
And don't want to be a bore.*

*So remember I do love you,
And wish that you were near.
Now it's nearly mail-time,
I must say goodbye, my dear.*

*Here I stand at the mail-box,
With face so very red.
Instead of mailing you my letter,
I have opened it instead!*

Eva Nielsen wrote this poem while in her late fifties when she was just "forgetful." Ironically, Alzheimer's disease later robbed her of her beautiful gift of poetry. And while we may smile at such illustrations about seniors' forgetfulness, to many of them (including the author!) the stories are not all that funny, as seniors seek to adjust to a failing memory. Interestingly, some seniors will demonstrate incredible long-term memory, but have difficulty recalling recent events and conversations.

9. Their most common emotional problem is probably depression.
10. If they outlive family members and friends, social isolation can become a major problem.
11. Many find security in clinging to familiar behavioral patterns, such as preferences for certain foods, routines, habits, etc.
12. For many, the most traumatic event of this age period is that dreaded time when their drivers' license is taken from them. Just as the acquisition of that license in the teen years served as a rite of passage into independence and adulthood, the loss of that license years later serves as a painful reminder that they have once again become dependent upon others.
13. Most of them now have the time for social activities and trips, but many will not have the funds nor health that will allow them to participate.
14. Retirement coming early in this period will bring a whole new set of adjustments, such as the wife now having a husband home all during the day. For many couples, this new arrangement is no problem, but others may possibly identify with the remark I once heard, "Retirement is having twice as much husband, but only half as much pay."
15. A long life, much of it spent in the costly "school of experience" can make many of these dear folks a rich storehouse of wisdom, waiting to be tapped by a younger generation.

Let me sum up this section by repeating the quotation with which I began it: "You are not teaching lessons; you are teaching people." If we ever hope to minister effectively to them, we must not forget this truth. Those are not just adult bodies sitting before you. They are people. Some of them are dealing with physical problems, such as a condition that will require surgery. Some are depressed. Some are struggling with temptation. Some are worried about a wayward child or a marriage that is falling apart. Does the Lord offer in His Word any guidance or principles that can help men and women cope with these types of problems? We will be addressing this question with Match #14.

DEFINITELY QUOTABLE:

"When I dig another out of trouble, the hole from which I lift him is the place where I bury my own." Chinese proverb

"If we want to move our world toward God, we need to learn to weep for them."

STRIKE THE MATCH:

Before you teach your adults next time, go back to the section above that profiles the particular age level you are teaching. Re-read it carefully and think of the individuals in your group. Make a mental note of some of the specific problems and needs these adults are facing now. Perhaps you may want to jot some of these needs down on your personal prayer list, and use this to guide your intercession for them. Finally, before you begin the preparation of each lesson, ask the Lord to use you and your teaching to help them handle effectively their problems and needs.

MATCH

8

LEARN AND USE THEIR NAMES

Years ago, I was out on church visitation one night, and my partner was Tom Jertberg, a married student at the College where I was teaching. Tom and I had been out several times together and had worked out a system, whereby we took turns introducing each other at the door. Well, this particular evening, as we approached the house, we agreed it was my turn. No problem. We rang the bell, and when the person opened the door, I said something like this: "Hi, we are here visiting from Salem Baptist Church. My name is Leonard Allred, and this is . . ." And at that point, as I turned to face Tom, my "computer screen" went black. Zip. Nothing. Graciously, Tom came to my rescue and filled in the blanks. Now, you might not be able personally to relate to a fiasco such as mine, but I'm sure that many of you have had the experience of meeting someone, exchanging names, shaking hands, and walking away, only to realize one minute later, you can't remember that person's name. Since I have a terrible problem remembering names (exhibit A: illustration above), I have been interested in any ideas that might help me improve my skills in this area. Here is a list I have been able to collect. I hope they will be as beneficial to you as they have to me.

1. Look into the person's face and give them your full attention; don't be looking over their shoulder at anyone or anything else that might be happening.
2. Concentrate on getting the name correctly. If in doubt, ask for correct spelling.

3. Use the name at once; if you don't get it right, your new acquaintance will probably correct you.
4. When appropriate, repeat the name several times during your conversation.
5. If possible, associate the name with some item or event which is familiar to you, but I can't guarantee this will work every time. Illustration. Years ago, I was in a church chatting with a man and trying to help him remember my name. In a stroke of sheer genius, I pointed to a red bench nearby and said, "My name is Allred, just like that bench." I left the church satisfied that I had settled that matter for time and eternity. Unfortunately, several days later I learned otherwise, when a friend was sharing with me how he had overheard that man in the church relate how he had met me. His words were something like these: "O yeah, I remember that guy. His name was Redbench." So much for the value of association!
6. Use the name again when you say goodbye.
7. After you have parted from the person, try to visualize the face and repeat the name.
8. Write down the name as soon as possible in your pocket calendar or palm pilot (if you are "high tech"). This process of spelling names will help fix them more permanently in your mind. At times I have written them in a little spiral pad, which I would carry with me everywhere I went. For instance, I had met this particular couple and recorded their names in my little book. I did not see them at church for months, and then one Sunday I spotted them across the church. I could not have remembered their names if I had been lined up and threatened with an assault rifle. But thankfully, I had my little book; so quickly pulling it out, I looked and found their names. Confidently armed with this knowledge, I walked up to where they were sitting and greeted them by name. They seemed quite impressed that I would remember them after such a long time. For some reason, I did not feel the compulsion to share the "secret" of my incredible memory!
9. Periodically look over the list of names you have recorded. Say aloud each name, trying at the same time to visualize the face.
10. If you are a teacher, make a prayer list of all your members (discussed with Match #3) and pray for them regularly, again visualizing each face as you do so. One of my friends, who had just assumed the position of youth pastor in a local church, took a group picture of all the teens in his group, enlarged the print, and wrote each teen's name

beside her/his picture.
11. If you meet a person later, but for some reason, you can't remember the name, what do you do? Well, don't bluff it and try to cover yourself by asking something like this, "And how do you spell your name?" The reply may be, "J-O-N-E-S." At that point, you are reasonably confident that you did something incredibly stupid. It is probably better, if you can't remember the name, to say something like this. "I am very sorry, but for some reason, I can't seem to recall your name." Most folks are very forgiving, and you will probably get by with this the first time. Just don't expect them to be that merciful the next fourteen times you forget their names!
12. When appropriate and if all else fails, providing name tags for all your adults, especially the visitors, may prove to be beneficial to everyone:
    a. They will obviously help your visitors who don't know the names of your members.
    b. They will help your members who don't know the names of the visitors; and possibly, if your group is large, may not know the names of some of the other members.
    c. Finally, they may even help you, as the teacher, on those days when you can't seem to remember anybody's name!

Summarily, PRACTICE! PRACTICE! PRACTICE! You may think you have a poor memory for names, but if you will diligently apply some of these suggestions, you will probably be pleasantly surprised how well they will work for you.

DEFINITELY QUOTABLE:

"And now among the fading embers, these in the main are my regrets. When I am right no one remembers, when I am wrong, no one forgets." Author unknown

"Others won't care how much we know until they know how much we care." Chuck Swindoll

STRIKE THE MATCH:

Review the list of suggestions above and experiment with some of them the next time you meet a visitor at church. Share the results of this experience with a good friend.

MATCH

9

PREPARE WELL FOR EACH LESSON

Have you ever had this experience? You drive by Restaurant A, and the parking lot is packed. Some of its customers, unable to be seated inside, are standing around outside the door. A little further down the street, you pass Restaurant B, and in its parking lot are five cars, belonging to the owner, the cook, and three waiters. What's the difference between these two restaurants? Probably a combination of the following factors. In Restaurant A the food is delicious, the prices are reasonable, and the servers are both pleasant and efficient. From this simple scenario comes a fairly obvious conclusion: you feed people well, and they will usually come back for more. And what is true for a restaurant serving physical food to its customers will generally be true for you as a teacher serving spiritual food to your adults. Feed them well, and they will probably return for more. But feeding them well is going to require a considerable investment of prayer and preparation on your part. Since I have already addressed the subject of prayer with Match #3, let me focus on sharing a few basic suggestions to guide you in preparing your lesson.

1. Begin preparation early enough. One faithful Sunday School teacher I knew years ago, would come home from church on Sunday morning, eat lunch, and that afternoon start studying for the next week's lesson. Recently I came across the statement of a Christian educator, who maintained that a minimum of between six to eight hours of preparation was necessary for teaching a lesson. But whether you are a Sunday School teacher or a professor teaching graduate level

courses in a Christian university, to be effective in the classroom is going to require some extensive time in preparation. Personally, I have spent more time as a college teacher preparing my lessons than I ever spent as a student preparing for my classes. One of the driving forces behind my emphasis on adequate preparation has been the statement, "If the teacher doesn't suffer before the lesson, the students will probably suffer during it."

2. Have some place set aside where you can study and prepare for your lessons. If you are a teacher on the college or graduate level, you will undoubtedly already have an office in which you can study and prepare for your classes; but if you are a Sunday school teacher, you may not have that luxury. Yet, even Sunday school teachers will need some place to study and keep their Bible study tools. Years ago, I knew a godly layman who had set aside one corner of his bedroom as a study area. However, four active children in the home at times made even that spot noisy, at which point he would retreat to his car, where he could pray and continue the preparation of his lesson.

3. Begin to collect those study tools which will be necessary for effective teaching. Let me illustrate the importance of this. You want to build an additional bedroom on your house. You go to the yellow pages and hire Joe Flugelhorn, a local contractor, to do the job. Next Monday, bright and early, Flugelhorn shows up at your home to start working, and the first thing he asks you is, "Say, can I borrow a hammer, saw, and some nails?" Your response? A "duh" and a quick trip back to the yellow pages! Just as a builder is going to need some basic tools if he is to be effective in his work, you too, as a teacher, will need certain basic tools if you want to be effective in your ministry. Now if you are a college/graduate school teacher, you will have been busy collecting such study tools since your undergraduate days. But even as a Sunday School teacher, there are certain basic tools you will need. Let me suggest a few:

    a. A good study Bible (with helpful notes and wide margins to take notes)
    b. A Bible concordance (ex. James Strong's *Exhaustive Concordance to the Bible*)
    c. A Bible dictionary (ex. *Unger's Bible Dictionary*)
    d. A Bible atlas (ex. *Baker's Bible Atlas*)

e. A Bible commentary (ex. *The Wycliffe Bible Commentary* edited by Pfeiffer and Harrison)

NOTE: Many times you will be able to find material on the internet or in some of the excellent software available today.

4. Seek to prepare your own heart spiritually
   a. Ask God to show you any unconfessed sins in your life and confess these to Him (and others, if necessary).
   b. Commit yourself afresh to the Lordship of Christ, asking Him to fill you with His Spirit
   c. Ask the Lord to help you become a consistent model of what He wants you and your adults to be.

5. STUDY! STUDY! STUDY! Know your material, and know more than you have time to teach. Someone said it well, "You can no more tell somebody something you don't know, than come back from some place you ain't been." That statement will probably earn an F for the grammar, but surely an A+ for its logic.

6. If you are teaching a Bible lesson, read carefully and prayerfully the Scripture passage(s) upon which the lesson is based. Look for truths (commands to obey, sins to avoid, promises to claim, etc.), that you need first to apply to your own life and then to the lives of your adults.

7. Begin collecting materials you can use with your lesson, such as contemporary news articles, quotations, illustrations, etc.

8. Prepare a lesson plan. If you are a Sunday School teacher, and using Biblically based materials produced by an Evangelical publisher, they will generally provide you with a teacher's manual, sometimes referred to as a quarterly. Consult that manual as you prepare for your lesson. Study the lesson plan suggested and use the ideas appropriate to your class, but also feel free to modify it to best meet the needs of your adults. But please "lose" that quarterly when you get up to teach. Few things will help send your adults into a stupor faster than standing in front of your class and reading a quarterly to them. I read about some teens who complained that their teacher was a "quarterly wired for sound." If you need to use some of the material in the quarterly, copy it into your outline, and keep your notes in your

Bible. For those of you who desire to develop your own lesson plans, you may want to read over the suggestions with the next Match. You may also find it helpful to check out Appendix B for a sample format to use in planning a lesson and then look through Appendix C, which is a sample plan actually completed and ready to use.

Summarily, adults appreciate competent, prepared teachers, who know their material and have the ability to communicate it decisively. May we, in the light of eternity, be willing to pay that price.

DEFINITELY QUOTABLE:

"By failing to prepare you are preparing to fail." Benjamin Franklin
"Our talk is often like a first draft; it usually needs a lot of corrections."
"The less one knows about a subject, the longer it will take to explain it."

STRIKE THE MATCH:

If you don't own some of the basic study tools mentioned above, make it a priority to purchase them. Or if you are "financially challenged", put them on your "wish list" for birthdays and Christmas, and let someone else pay for them!

MATCH

10

MAKE A LESSON PLAN

Let me start off this section by going back to Joe Flugelhorn, mentioned in the scenario under the last Match. He arrives at your house and never even asks you about your plans for this new bedroom. He just starts sawing wood and nailing pieces together. "Duh" again! No, you would go over with him exactly what you want done: location of door and windows, walls, receptacles, type of floor covering, etc. He needs a plan if he is to do the job right. And just as an architect needs a blueprint, or a cook needs a recipe, many teachers have found it essential to have a lesson plan. Obviously, there is no one way to format a lesson plan. Through the years of teaching adults in workshops and Sunday school, I have found one plan that has worked well for me. In Appendix C, mentioned under the last Match, you will find a sample which I was privileged to use several years ago when teaching a class of adults. While this sample is somewhat lengthy, you may find it helpful to refer to it as we walk through the following suggestions for preparing a lesson.

1. Select an appropriate title.
2. List the Scripture text(s) upon which the lesson is based.
3. Name your target group (ex. young marrieds).
4. Write in the date and place you are teaching this lesson (ex. Salem Baptist Church on August 24, 2003). This information may prove to be very helpful to you later if full-blown dementia sets in, and you can't remember what country you were living in when you taught this lesson!

5. Select a lesson aim. When formulating such an aim, it is important to keep in mind that it should be (1) brief enough to be remembered, (2) clear enough to be written, and (3) realistic enough to be achieved.
6. Make a checklist of all the items you will need for the lesson, begin collecting them, and be sure to go over this list before you leave home.
7. Plan an introduction that will "grab" their attention. See Match #11 for some ideas.
8. Outline your lesson content in the order in which you will be presenting it and indicate places where you intend to insert your methods, illustrations, and applications.
9. Select the teaching methods you will be using. You should show in your lesson where you plan to use each method and also any notes you need to remember as you use it. A list of methods suitable for adults, along with suggestions on how to use them, is found with Match #16.
10. Think of specific ways the truths of the lesson can be applied to the everyday lives of your adults. Make these applications throughout the lesson; do not just tack an application on the end, like a postscript, which incidentally may signal many of your adults to unplug their input line before you stop transmitting!
11. Allow some time at the end to review briefly the major points of the lesson and to make a final application and/or challenge.

DEFINITELY QUOTABLE:

"If I take care of my character, my reputation will take care of itself."
D.L. Moody

STRIKE THE MATCH:

Check out the sample lesson plan mentioned above, at least to familiarize yourself with its location. The next time you are preparing a lesson for teaching a group of adults, you might want to revisit this sample and hopefully find some useful ideas for your teaching.

MATCH

11

GRAB AND KEEP THEIR ATTENTION

The story is fictitious, old, and the details a bit blurred in my memory, but it makes a good point. It seems that a farmer was trying to sell his mule, and he was bragging to the prospective buyer about the animal's intelligence. The highlight of his sales pitch was, "All you have to do is just speak to him, and he will obey you." Impressed, the man bought the mule and headed home. When he arrived there, he thought it would be a good idea to try out his skill in communicating with his newly purchased friend. But to his dismay, none of his directives seemed to impress the mule, who stood absolutely unmoved by the most frantic efforts of his new owner. Disturbed and angry, the man brought the mule back to the former owner and said, "I thought you said, all I had to do was just speak to this mule, and he would obey me!" The farmer never said a word, picked up a piece of wood, whacked it across the mule's head, and said calmly to the startled man, "You gotta get his attention first!"

And so it is with adults. If you are going to teach them (not just talk to them), "you gotta get their attention." Now, I don't personally recommend using a 2x4 piece of wood to make this happen. There is a better way, and we will be looking at a few suggestions later. But for right now, we need to define a couple of important terms. First, what is attention? A couple of definitions that work for me are "the act or state of applying the mind to an object" and "mental concentration." O.K., now what is meant by the term, attention span? One suggestion is that it is the length of time an individual can stay focused on a subject before his mind begins to wander. And just what is the attention span of an average adult? Good question. No one knows for sure. There are just too many variables that could affect it. The list could probably include extremes in room temperature, how well you are prepared (don't expect them to stay tuned if you keep your face buried in your teacher's manual that you first looked at that morning during breakfast), the spiritual and/or physical condition of your adults, and the subject matter of the lesson. Let me park for a moment on that last item.

Let's talk about Wilbur Dinglebat. On Super Bowl Sunday, Wilbur, an NFL addict, is glued to the TV set for three to four hours, making brief "pit stops" only to go to the bathroom or the refrigerator. This particular Sunday each year is a very hazardous time for wives, children, and other valuable possessions. For example, his wife could have a stroke, his children could be kidnapped, and his new car stolen, and he probably wouldn't know it until after the last play of the game. Why? It's really very simple. He is absorbed in the subject matter being pumped into his living room that particular day. Now, take Wilbur and sit him down in your Sunday school class, and on a particular Sunday morning lecture on the identity of the right big toe of Nebuchadnezzar's image in the second chapter of Daniel. What is going to happen? Probably about three minutes into your lesson, Wilbur is going to set his body on "automatic pilot," and his mind is going to check out. It is not surprising, then, that Christian educators for years have been maintaining that if you are going to teach individuals, you must gain and sustain their attention. So, let's think about how you can make this happen.

Years ago, I was teaching a class on Principles and Methods of Teaching, and as a requirement for the course, each student had to teach a lesson to the rest of the class. Since I had tried to emphasize to these college students the importance of gaining attention at the beginning of their lessons, I was prepared to grade them on their ability to do that. But I was not quite prepared for this one young lady, who stood up, raised a glass in her hand, and threw it to the wooden floor, sending glass shrapnel in all directions! I don't recommend her method, but she definitely grabbed our attention. Well, aside from threatening the lives of your adults with flying glass, what can you do to get their attention at the beginning of your lesson? Here are a few suggestions that you might want to try, which have been very productive for other teachers:

1. Audio-visuals, such as PowerPoint, overhead projector, or even a simple object lesson.
2. A brief story that is relevant to the lesson.
3. A question, not a "no brainer" that will call for a simple yes or no, but one that will challenge and stretch their minds. Perhaps you might want to print a question on the dry erase board before class begins, so they can be thinking about it as they enter the room. For example, you might use the question, "Do your beliefs affect your behavior?"
4. A humorous incident.
5. A role play.
6. An assignment, such as announcing to your class members the topic of the lesson and asking them to look up and write down as many Scripture verses as they could find which they felt pertained to that topic.
7. Or any teaching method that is relevant to your subject and aim. See ideas under Match #16.

O.K., so you have been successful in grabbing their attention. Now what? You soon discover that you must fight to keep it. If you don't, you will probably find yourself looking into some faces that have a very blank expression. They are looking right at you, but they have already left the room. You know, it's like "the lights are on, but no one is home." So how do you keep their attention? Very simple. During your lesson, you need to keep using some of the same methods that you used to gain it initially. Role plays, stories, and visuals will all help you "round up" those straying minds and regain their attention, providing of course, that these remedies don't come too late, and some of your class members have not already lapsed into a vegetative state.

DEFINITELY QUOTABLE:

"There are five Gospels - Matthew, Mark, Luke, John, and the Christian. And some people will never read the first four." Gypsy Smith

STRIKE THE MATCH:

Reread the section above and then look over the methods discussed under Match #16. Try out a new method to introduce your next lesson that will grab your adults' attention. If it works, and you are really brave, plan to use other new ones to sustain that attention during your lesson.

MATCH

12

SHOW THEM WHY THEY NEED THE MATERIAL YOU ARE TEACHING THEM

Some time ago in one of my college classes, a student raised his hand and asked, "Can I ask you a question?" Pleased that he wanted to be involved this way in the lesson, I shot back confidently, "Sure, go ahead." But I wasn't quite ready for his particular question. It went something like this, "Why are we studying this stuff?" I'm still trying to dig that dagger out from between my second and third ribs! But in his question he actually did me a favor, for at that moment he made me painfully aware that I had done a lousy job of selling him (and probably the rest of the class) on the importance of the material we were discussing that day. You see, it is not all that complicated. You will not be very interested in buying a lawnmower from me if you don't have any grass. And your adults will probably not be very interested in your lesson material if they don't see their need of it. They appreciate Bible study that is relevant to their needs and useful immediately, or at least in the near future. And this brings us to the subject of motivation. Again, we need to define some terms. A good dictionary definition of motive is "a need or desire that causes a person to act." If we accept that definition, it should follow logically that to motivate is "to supply a reason for acting." Translating all this into the classroom, we may conclude that our effectiveness in teaching adults will be directly related to our skills in motivating them to learn.

For years Christian educators have recognized two basic types of motivation. They may give them different names, but for our purposes, we will simply refer to them as intrinsic (internal) and extrinsic (external) motivation. Let's talk about each of them briefly in the context of adult education.

First, with extrinsic motivation, adults are learning because the teacher has introduced secondary incentives. If you are teaching in a college or graduate school, you soon discover that not all of your students will come running into your classrooms, turn their eager faces to you, and cry out in unison, "O teacher, we love you and all this material. Please start teaching us now. We can hardly wait." Yeah . . . in your dreams! If you are teaching college students, you will find that some of them are genuinely, intrinsically motivated, especially the older, mature students. But for most of them, you will need to apply varying forms of external pressure to motivate them to take notes and learn the material. This external pressure (extrinsic motivation) will take the form of pop quizzes, exams, grades, and possibly for those who do not respond to these, academic probation and failure. Obviously such measures will not work when you are teaching adults in a local church educational situation, Sunday school, or a home Bible study. For example, it might not be the sharpest idea to offer candy bars to adults who memorized the Bible verse of the week, or try to keep after class all those who may have failed to study their lesson beforehand. And that brings me to the second type of motivation, intrinsic.

In intrinsic motivation, adults want to learn because they recognize that the lesson content will be valuable to them, both now and in the future. But the BIG question is how do you communicate that fact to your class? Let me offer a few suggestions:

1. Take a few minutes at the beginning of your lesson to explain how they will need the material you will be presenting. I have been told of one well known seminary professor who would take a considerable amount of time during the first class of his course to explain to his students why they would need this particular course in their lives and ministries. Going back to the lesson plan shown in APPENDIX C, it might be good to take a couple of minutes before you get into your lesson to say to your adults something like this: "Today, we are going to be looking at some types of sins which are committed against

the Holy Spirit of God. Sadly, it is possible for even Christians to be guilty of some of these sins. I have known some of these believers personally, and to my knowledge, they are still reaping the harvest of those sins, having lost their testimonies, their marriages, and their ministries. The burden of my heart today is that this will not happen to any of you in this class." It should be our prayer that the Spirit will use words such as these to grab the attention of those believers in your class and motivate them to listen to and heed the truths you will be sharing with them.

2. Love your adults and demonstrate this, in and out of class, by seeking to minister to their needs and problems. One Christian educator put it this way: "Scratch them where they itch." If your adults sense that you really care about them and their welfare (spiritually, physically, emotionally, etc.), I believe they will be far more motivated to listen attentively to you and seriously consider your instruction.

3. Encourage their input in selecting topics to be discussed in class. I will say more about this with the next Match.

DEFINITELY QUOTABLE:

"Education is the process of passing from unconscious ignorance to conscious ignorance." Louis Sperry Chafer

STRIKE THE MATCH:

As you look over the contents of your next lesson for your adults, ask yourself the question, "Do they really need to know this stuff?" If you are convinced that they do, think up some creative way, preferably before you get into your actual lesson, or shortly after you do so, to sell them on that fact.

MATCH

13

INVITE THEIR INPUT IN SELECTING TOPICS FOR STUDY

If you are currently teaching an adult Sunday school class, you probably are using curriculum materials from an Evangelical publisher. But even as I type these words, I can hear some Christians objecting, "We don't use curriculum materials. They are just man's opinions. We teach the Bible." Now as spiritual as that statement may seem at first, I think it has several serious flaws.

1. Most of those who voice such complaints probably do not have the academic credentials or ministry experience necessary to prepare lessons that would approximate the quality of some of the Christian educational materials available today.

2. Writing good curriculum is extremely time consuming. This is time that I feel could be spent more profitably in other ways, such as praying for your class members, visiting them in their homes, preparing a meal for a sick person, or even going out with someone for a "McDonald's break." Somebody back there had it right, when they said, "There's no need to re-invent the wheel."

3. I have not been extremely impressed by some of those who claim "we are just teaching the Bible." In many cases, this "teaching the Bible" actually consists of lecturing (often preaching) through a pas-

age, "persecuting" one verse and then "fleeing" to the next!

4. Those who object to materials, because they just contain man's opinions, actually end up doing the same thing, just substituting their opinions and interpretations for those of others.

Summarily, I think that there is published material available today that you could use very effectively, keeping in mind that you may have to modify it somewhat to meet the precise needs of your adults. If your church is not presently using some type of published Christian curriculum, and if you live in an area that has a Christian book store, why not go by there and check out some of the samples they will probably have on display?

However, as great as any material may be, there is no way that its writers, no matter how well qualified, could ever fully anticipate where your adults are, spiritually, emotionally, socially, and intellectually. Furthermore, many adults like to have a voice in selecting what they will be studying. For example, they may have questions about topics such as the creation vs. evolution debate, evidences for Noah's flood, guidelines for improving relationships in their families, or maybe handling the belief system of those pesky cultists who show up at the door fairly regularly. Some of your members may even express to you their interest in studying such issues, but unfortunately the majority of them will never let you know this. How, then, can you as a teacher discover and speak to some of their underlying areas of concern which may not be addressed in your curriculum materials? Let me share a couple of suggestions that have worked well for some Sunday school teachers.

1. Distribute 3x5 cards to your adults and ask them to list two or three topics they would like to see discussed in class. On the basis of their responses, figure out some way to deal with these in future lessons. If there is sufficient interest in a particular subject, consider the possibility of perhaps offering a ten to twelve week course dealing with it.

2. Prepare a "Hot Box," perhaps a shoe box covered with red paper. Cut a slot in the top and place it at the back of your classroom. Inform your class that if they have any questions concerning the Bible, just to write them down on a piece of paper and drop them into the box, and you will take a few minutes each Sunday before your lesson to

address one of their questions. Inform them that it is not necessary for them to sign their names to the notes.

3. Suggest the possibility of grouping your adult Sunday school classes by areas of their social interests and needs. Such an arrangement could create a class for each of the following groups:

   a. Young, unmarried singles: Unfortunately today, many churches have a dynamite youth ministry, but when their seniors graduate from high school, the only option the church has for them is a married couples class. Now, let's face it, no high school graduate is going to get terribly excited about sitting in a room full of couples talking about changing pampers and burping babies. Regardless of the state of your ministry to your teens, you definitely need a vibrant class for these young singles. Older singles (unmarried, divorced, and widowed) can be integrated into co-ed classes in their age brackets.
   b. Couples without children
   c. Parents with preschool children
   d. Parents with elementary age children
   e. Parents of teens (One church offered a class made up primarily of parents of teens, and a class member observed, "For the first time in many years, I felt a strong need to be in Sunday school.")
   f. Empty nesters (Another church started a class for this group and soon had 50 adults attending; many of whom had not been coming to Sunday school prior to that.)
   g. Single parents (Is your church ready to welcome that unmarried mom or dad, with one or two small children, who shows up at your church next Sunday?)

   One evident problem with arrangements c, d, e would be which class parents would attend if the ages of their children ranged across several of the categories shown above? Since most parents come up a bit short in the area of omnipresence, they will just have to choose which class best meets their needs and those of their children.

4. Consider the possibility of offering adult electives. In case some of you may not be familiar with this concept. Let me explain briefly how it works. In a Sunday school, these are courses that would be offered quarterly on the basis of the adults' interest. In some churches their entire adult department studies electives. Other churches,

probably the majority, will want most of their teachers to teach the regular adult curriculum during a quarter, but allow one or two teachers to make available certain electives, which are taught during that same time period. Adults are given the opportunity to attend the class of their choice, and at the end of the quarter, they may return to their original class. If you think this idea has merit in your situation, and your adults would be in favor of it, discuss it with your Senior Pastor and the Sunday school leaders. Although they may not want the entire Sunday school to shift to this elective system, they may allow you to use it in your class, at least for a quarter. If so, probably the next step would be to prepare a handout to distribute to your members. Here are some guidelines for you in preparing this.

a. Make a list of all the topics that you feel would interest your particular class. This list could be generated from a survey of your adults. It probably would be a good idea to include with each subject a brief description of the contents you plan to cover in that elective (see sample below).
b. Just to the left of each topic place a short line or box as a place for your adults who may be interested in that course to indicate their level of interest in it.
c. When you distribute this handout, ask your class to look over the list of topics and then rank their top five choices, using 1 for the subject of most interest to them.
d. Use the results of this survey to determine the topics that you will be offering and the sequence you will follow in presenting them.
e. IMPORTANT NOTE: Before you place any elective on this list, be sure that there are materials available, and be sure you feel competent to teach that subject. If there is a particular subject that seems especially popular with your adults, and yet you don't feel exactly comfortable tackling it, you may want to bring this to the attention of your Sunday school leadership. They may agree to allow you to bring in another church member as a resource person to teach part, if not all, of that elective. In some instances you may be able to locate an excellent series using either VHS or DVD format that will address this topic.

Here is a list of possible adult electives:

Bible Doctrine - Surveys the basic fundamentals of the Christian faith

Personal Evangelism - Discusses procedure in soulwinning and suggests ways to deal with some of the basic problems and excuses encountered

Principles and Methods of Bible Study - Deals with some of the basic principles that will enable believers both to interpret the Bible and apply its truths to their lives

Cults - Discusses and evaluates, from a Scriptural perspective, the basic tenets of some of the more well known cults, such as Jehovah Witnesses, Mormons, and Seventh Day Adventists

Occult - Discusses and evaluates, from a Scriptural perspective, the teachings of Witchcraft, Satanism, Spiritualism, and Astrology

Evidences for Believing the Bible is God's Word - Discusses fulfilled prophecy, archaeology, the unity of the Bible, etc.

Evidences for the Universal Flood - Discusses both Biblical and extra-Biblical evidences

The Christian Home - Discusses, from a Biblical perspective, love, roles of the husband and wife, finances, and the training of children

Creationism vs Evolution - Discusses both models and demonstrates the Biblical and extra-Biblical evidences for Creationism (including the Intelligent Design movement)

Church History - Traces in broad strokes the history of the church from the Book of Acts to the present time.

DEFINITELY QUOTABLE:

"The seven last words of a dying church: We never did it that way before."

STRIKE THE MATCH:

Pray for your adults and ask the Lord to help you find the most effective way to minister to their interests and needs. Don't be afraid to try something different. If you can't think of anything at first, try one of those ideas listed above. The Hot Box would probably be a good place to start, and fairly easy to implement. I believe you will find that the more you are interested in listening to them and their needs, the more they will be interested in listening to you.

MATCH

14

HELP THEM APPLY GOD'S TRUTH TO THEIR LIVES

It was Sunday morning and my wife and I were listening to a guest preacher in our church. From my past contacts with him, I believe he loved the Lord and was sincerely seeking to honor and serve Him. His message was Biblically sound. His sermon was well-organized. His preaching style was not spectacular, but it kept most of us awake. Yet, the more I listened that morning, the more I became aware that something extremely vital was missing. He never made any effort to connect the Biblical truths in his sermon with the lives of the people in the pews. So while I sat there, I started thinking about those individuals sitting near us. Since I thought it might be a bit distracting if I stood up and did a complete 360 degree turn, I just focused on the ones I could see by looking ahead or with my peripheral vision. I took a piece of paper and began to jot down their names, and very soon I had seven or eight individuals on my list. Now, this happened a number of years ago, and I cannot remember the exact people or the particular problems that each of them was wrestling with that morning. So taking the liberty to change names and details, let me share with you a few of their stories.

There was Ted, fighting a continuing battle with heart problems and seeking to minister to his dear wife who had been diagnosed with cancer. There was Jessica, seeking to keep her testimony and be a good wife to an unsaved, hostile husband. There was Lisa, confined to a wheelchair for the rest of her life. There were Barry and Valerie, seeking to cope with a rebellious teenage son. There was Tricia, an unmarried mother, now a Christian, seeking to rear a daughter for the Lord. There was Chad, who had just recently buried his dear wife after twenty-five years of a great marriage. There was Juanita, a widow, whose health was deteriorating because of rheumatoid arthritis. And those were only the ones I could see. Only Heaven fully understood the heartaches and problems present that Sunday morning. And yet that preacher, throughout his thirty minute sermon, never made one attempt to apply its truths to the lives and hurts of those who sat before him. Sadly, this scenario has been multiplied innumerable times, not just in our pulpits, but also in our classrooms. It almost seems as if preachers and teachers today operate according to one or the other of the following models, which I have decided to name the Information Model or the Integration Model. Surely, such titles don't exactly represent awesome creativity on my part, but I trust they will communicate what's on my heart concerning this issue. Let me try to characterize briefly each of these models, restricting my remarks to the context of a teacher ministering to a group of adults.

In the Information Model the emphasis is on just that - information. Translated into a Christian context, the teacher is basically concerned about "teaching the Bible" which usually eventuates in a steady stream of facts (ex. the exact distance from Jerusalem to Jericho), doctrines (ex. a thoroughly Biblical treatment of sanctification), the faithful retelling of a familiar Biblical narrative (ex. the story of Nehemiah leading the Jews back home to Israel, complete with all the historical dates), a well documented refutation of a heresy (ex. looking at the tenets of Jehovah Witnesses from a Biblical perspective), or the interpretation of a Scripture passage (ex. Romans 8:28-30, being very careful to relate what the term "predestinate" means in the "the original language"). Is all of this important? Of course, it is. So, what's the problem? Lest you think I just got up on the wrong side of the bed this morning in a particularly negative mood, let me share with you what I consider to be two critical flaws in this Model of teaching.

1. The Information Model of teaching gives relatively little consideration to the ultimate purpose of God giving us His revelation of truth found in His Word. He did not give us His truth just to read or hear it and then frame it in our doctrinal statement. No, He gave us His truth

that we might believe it and bring our lives into conformity to paraphrasing a quotation I heard, "God wants us to believe the truth but He also wants us to behave the truth." This principle seems to be supported by a number of Scriptures. Let me mention a few, just from the New Testament. Jesus did not say to His disciples, "If ye know these things, happy [or blessed] are ye if ye underline them in your Bible, or memorize them, or recite them, or even include them in your doctrinal statement." No, He said, ". . . happy [or blessed] are ye if ye do them" (John 13:17). Paul, writing to his beloved Timothy, said, "Now the end [or purpose] of the commandment [or instruction] is charity [or love] out of a pure heart, and of a good conscience, and of faith unfeigned" (I Timothy 1:5). Paul's ultimate purpose for his teaching was not knowledge stored in the head, but knowledge that transformed the life. James wrote, "But be ye doers of the Word, and not hearers only, deceiving your own selves." (James 1:22). And then he proceeded in that familiar passage to warn of the danger of hearing the truth and not being obedient to it. From these passages and others, it would seem fairly clear that when teachers become absorbed in just transmitting truth to their classes, they are missing God's ultimate purpose for giving us that truth.

2. This model fails to give adequate consideration to the make-up of man. For years, Christian educators have recognized that individuals possess not only intellect but also emotion and will. Therefore, if you as a teacher of adults want to make a maximum impact on their lives, you must address all three of these areas in your teaching. You do need to appeal to their intellect, and this does involve giving them information. Unfortunately, too many teachers stop here. You also need to speak to their emotions, and then appeal to their wills, showing them how God's truths should be applied to their lives. Personally, I like a teacher who stretches me intellectually, stimulates me emotionally (makes me cry and/or laugh), and challenges me to do something with the truth that has been shared.

And this brings us to a consideration of the Integration Model. In this model, the teacher remains committed to a Biblical worldview and faithful exposition of the Scriptures in transmitting information (Biblical and extra-Biblical truths), but also remembering God's ultimate purpose for giving us truth, discussed above, seeks to integrate that truth, particularly

Biblical truth, into the everyday lives of adults. For years, Christian educators have referred to this as helping students to see how God's truth needs to be applied to their lives, hence the title of this Match. This will necessitate, on the teacher's part, a continuing alertness, not only to recognize those truths that can be applicable to adults, but also to show them how to respond to those truths in faith and obedience. There are at least two critical areas where you, as a teacher, should be trying to make this happen.

Clearly, the first area would be in your classroom. As you study the Scriptures that you will be sharing with your adults, look for those points in the lesson where you can make applications to their lives. Of course, not all passages in the Word will lend themselves to easy application. For instance, if you find yourself in I Chronicles, chapters 1-9, you will probably find it just a bit difficult to find much there that would be applicable to adults living in this century. Difficult, but not impossible. Actually, there are some tremendous nuggets tucked away in those chapters that you would do well to bring to the attention of your adults. I like to refer to them as "Gems from the Genealogies." Examples? Look at 1:44, where we read, "And when Bela was dead, Jobab the son of Zerah of Bozrah reigned in his stead." Application? No matter how much we think we are indispensable ("What would this church do without me?"), actually when we pass off the scene, there will always be a Jobab to take our place. The truth of the matter is that when we die, most of the world will not even know we are gone! Or look also at 6:15, where we read, "And Jehozadak went into captivity, when the Lord carried away Judah and Jerusalem by the hand of Nebuchadnezzar." Application? God still uses even sinful rulers to accomplish His eternal, perfect plan. That's probably a great truth for us as believers to remember today!

Most of the time, you should not have problems spotting points where you can make good applications of the lesson to the lives of your adults. For instance, if your lesson is dealing with Matthew 8:18-27, look at verse 18, where we read, "Now when Jesus saw great multitudes about Him, He gave commandment to depart unto the other side." Note: Jesus did not say, let's get into the boat and go out to the middle of the lake and drown! He said, let's go to the other side! Application? Sometimes in the midst of those trials of life, such as persecution, chronic illness, and staggering medical bills, we need to remember that Jesus is going to get us to the other side, either helping us get through these trials, or one day taking us home to be with Him, where all our trials will be over. Then look also at verse 23, where we see, "And when He was entered into a ship, His disciples followed Him." Note: Jesus was with His disciples, even in the midst of the horrific storm that soon overtook them there on the Sea of Galilee. Application? Our Lord never promised to keep us from the storms of life, such as sickness or loss of a loved one, but He did promise to be with us and give us His grace in those storms. Check out His wonderful promise in Hebrews 13:5.

You might even ask your adults to find the truths that they need to apply to their lives. One Sunday school teacher gave a class of middle-aged adults the following assignment. They were to read Ephesians 4:31, 32 and Philippians 4:6-8. They were asked to paraphrase these passages, trying not to use any of the words of the text. When they had finished that, they were to write out several scenarios of everyday life, in which they would need to apply the truths in these passages to their lives.

Then in addition to allowing your class to make applications of Biblical truths to their lives, challenge them to do this on their own in their daily quiet time. One of the greatest helps to me personally in this area has been SPECT, an acronym for the following:

S   sin to avoid
P   promise to claim
E   example to follow
C   command to obey
T   thanksgiving (for example, the account of Jesus' causing the blind man to see should make us thankful for the precious gift of our eyesight)

Encourage your adults to jot this acronym down on a 3x5 card, place it in their Bible to mark where they are in their daily reading, and use it this way. When they find a sin they should avoid, for example, grieving the Holy Spirit (Ephesians 4:30), they can underline that verse and place an S next to that verse in the margin. When they find a promise to claim, for example, God's promise to supply all our needs (Philippians 4:19), encourage them to underline that verse and place a P next to it in the margin. When you explain this plan to your class, you can give them examples of the remaining three points. But any time they use this procedure in marking these verses, remind them to stop right then and pray for the Lord to help them walk in the light He has just shared with them.

Summarily, this discussion of the approach to teaching, which I have termed the Integration Model, was never intended to be comprehensive. Hopefully, it will serve as a catalyst to challenge you as a teacher of adults, if you are not already doing so, to implement it in your teaching.

DEFINITELY QUOTABLE:

"Not many people care what happened to the Jebusites, but they desperately need to know how they can keep their homes intact."
Warren Wiersbe
"Many people search the Bible, but few let the Bible search them."

STRIKE THE MATCH:

If you, as a teacher, have not been in the habit of doing this, let me suggest that as you study your next lesson, try to think of your adults, with their needs and problems. Then look for truths in your lesson, and ways in which your class members can see how these truths may be applied to their lives. Mark these places in your notes. You may even want to write out what you plan to say to when you make these applications.

MATCH

15

BE SURE YOU ARE COMMUNICATING

If you started off your next lesson by writing on the board, "The trebucket was broken," what would be the responses of your adults? After using this little experiment for years, I think I can tell you that their responses will be varied. Some will look puzzled. Some will question you concerning the meaning of the sentence (unless they are somewhat conversant in the French language). Some may even question your sanity. What is my point? In this statement you have used an unfamiliar word with them, and consequently what we know as communication has come to a screeching halt. Sadly, we as teachers make this same mistake repeatedly with our adults. We use terms, especially good Biblical terms, such as justification, regeneration, and propitiation and just assume that our listeners understand their meanings. And while some of them will understand, some will not. And sadly, those who don't understand will probably never let you know it, for fear of being embarrassed over their ignorance. Bottom line? Many times we may be talking, but possibly not communicating. So, what is communication? Rather than giving a generic, dictionary definition of the word, let me suggest that it is the process of getting an idea from my mind to yours so that you understand exactly what I mean. Unfortunately, this process does not always work as efficiently as we may think it has.

From the world of childhood comes the following. His eyes tightly shut, the little boy finished his bedtime prayer with this request, "Bless Mommy and Daddy, Harold," and then in a quick postscript, continued,

"Please make grandma well." His mother gasped, "Harold? Who's he?" With some surprise on his face, her son looked up and asked, "Why, don't you know? That's God. We learned His name in Sunday school. Our Father which art in heaven, Harold be thy name". I doubt seriously if that boy's teacher ever realized that the communication process had broken down. And possibly you, as a teacher, may not realize it either. If communication is to happen in a classroom, several components must be in place and functioning correctly.

1. The Sender (you, the teacher)
2. The Message (the information you want to impart)
3. The Medium (the teacher's choice concerning the most effective way to encode that information, such as words, visuals, or some type of body language)
4. The Receiver (the student)
5. Interpretation (the process whereby the student decodes the Message, or information, which you have sent)
6. Feedback (the response given by the Receiver to the Sender)

If communication, by the definition given above, is to take place between you and your adults, they must interpret accurately the message you have sent. Perhaps one of the most critical factors in this entire process is that you as the teacher must use a medium that is familiar to them. For example, in the illustration given above, I have an idea that I can readily visualize in my head. "The trebuchet is broken." I know the meaning of that statement, but I have verbally encoded that idea with a medium of communication (a term) that is unfamiliar to my receivers. They don't know the meaning of the word. Hence, I failed to communicate. This same principle will hold true in the use of visuals, such as those icons which adorn the desktop of our computers. If you are not familiar with the meaning of that icon, communication between you and your computer is going to come to an abrupt end.

But let's go back briefly to that seventh factor, feedback. This is the response your adults will be giving you the entire time you are teaching your lesson. It will come in the form of a number of different "signals," which may include a smile, a soft "Amen," nodding in agreement, asking questions, doodling on a piece of paper, sleeping, or shaking their watches. I tell my classes that I don't mind too much if they look at their watches, but it does bother me if they shake them vigorously or tap them to be sure they are still working! Should you as a teacher be concerned about this feedback you are receiving from your adults? Definitely, unless you just have a fascination with listening to yourself talk. A critical question that arises at this point is how can you determine if you are actually communicating to them and they are interpreting accurately the messages you are sending? Let me mention a few suggestions.

1. Avoid or explain carefully any terms you suspect may be unfamiliar to your adults (not in a condescending way that seems to indicate you consider them all to be brain damaged). This will be especially important to remember when you venture into the area of theology, which has its own particular glossary. And by the way, don't ever use a term that you can't define. I confess I am often tempted to use a word that will make me sound extremely intelligent, even though I have no idea what it means. If I go ahead and use it in class, guess what happens? Some student will invariably ask, "What does that word mean?" Results? I squirm, sweat, and pray for the Rapture! Seriously, when I plan to use a term in my lesson, but am concerned that I won't remember its meaning, I write out the definition in my notes.

2. When you introduce a new term, stop and ask someone to define it. I have found it helpful to remind myself to ask this question by writing beside that term in my notes the words, "define term?" You can either throw this question out to the all of your adults or ask a particular individual, and using that answer, guide the rest of your group to a correct understanding of the term. And by the way, unless you have a bus load of Ph.D.'s in the room, you may want to lose the idea of using those six-syllable words, which will probably impress a small number of your adults but mystify the rest. Usually, it is best to stick to simple words that everyone can understand.

3. Watch their faces. If they register puzzlement or confusion, it's probably time to stop the tape, rewind, and go over the material again.

4. Occasionally ask an individual to paraphrase some truth you have just shared. It could be a verse in the passage you are studying or a statement you have just made. What is a paraphrase? It is a restatement of a text, giving the meaning in different words. For example,

you have just explained to your adults the meaning of the verse, "Pray without ceasing" (I Thessalonians 5:17). Stop right there, and ask someone to paraphrase this verse, or give it back it to you in his or her own words. If the respondents can do this correctly, it demonstrates to you that at least those individuals have comprehended the meaning of the verse, and you have communicated successfully. By the way, in your last class, did you just talk or communicate?

P.S. FOR THE EYES OF THE CURIOUS ONLY: a trebucket was a medieval war engine used to hurl stones and similar missiles at the enemy.

DEFINITELY QUOTABLE:

"Nothing is opened more often by mistake than the mouth." Author unknown

STRIKE THE MATCH:

Beginning with your next lesson, cultivate the habit of carefully looking over your notes for any term that you feel may be unfamiliar to your adults. Either substitute a more familiar word with the same meaning, or find some interesting way to define it.

MATCH

16

USE A VARIETY OF TEACHING METHODS

What is the worst teaching method you can use with adults? Possibly some will suggest the lecture, due to the criticism it has received in recent years. But probably the worst teaching method is, as someone so aptly remarked, "the one you use all the time." As an illustration, I have a good friend who was the teacher of a young adult Sunday school class. For some reason, he became enamored with the Buzz group method, and proceeded to employ that method just about every Sunday. Needless to say, many of the adults in his class soon became very discontented and no longer shared his passion for it. It has been my conviction for years that if you as a teacher wish to have maximum impact upon your adults, you will need to use some variety in your methodology. Thankfully, a number of options are available. Several years ago I came across a chart listing 57 teaching methods. Of that number, 35 were shown as being appropriate for use in teaching adults. Some of these, according to my experience and observation of other teachers, have been particularly effective. Here are some of my favorites, which I trust will become helpful to you.

1. Agree - Disagree. In this method you would make a certain statement to your adults. An illustration would be, "If Christian parents have one or more of their children grow up to rebel against them and God and adopt a sinful lifestyle, it is evidence that those parents did something wrong in the child-rearing process." Then ask those in

your group who agree with that statement to raise their hands. Then ask those who disagree to raise their hands. At that point, you could proceed to allow these two groups, one at a time, to speak and give the reasons for their responses. After a reasonable amount of time and after both sides have been given the opportunity to make their views known, try to sum up their arguments and draw some conclusions. Just as an observation, I think preachers, by making statements similar to the one above, have done serious damage to those parents who really have done the best job they could in rearing their children to live for God, but apparently were unsuccessful. Such preaching serves only to add more pain to those who already have been punishing themselves over their perceived failures. I find it most interesting that the Bible gives us numerous examples of apparently good parents who had horrific results with their children. And by the way, how many of us feel qualified to blame God for Adam and Eve's moral meltdown in the garden?

2. Audio-visuals. (discussed later with Match #20)

3. Brainstorming. In this method, you would announce a topic or question to be "stormed" or discussed. For example, in your lesson you are talking about temptation, and you come to I Corinthians 10:13, "There hath no temptation taken you but such as is common to man; but God is faithful, Who will not suffer you to be tempted above that ye are able; but will with the temptation also make a way to escape, that ye may be able to bear it." At that point ask your adults to share "ways of escape" that God has provided and that have worked for them in escaping temptation. As they relate these ideas, list them on the board. Do not allow any criticism of an idea when it is given. At the end of this listing, discuss their ideas, evaluate them, and seek to draw some conclusions.

4. Buzz groups. Divide your adults into smaller groups. There is no sacred number for the size of each group, but they should be kept small enough to allow all the members to participate. The number of groups will depend on the total number present. My experience has been that this method is not very effective if you have less than 10 or more than 40 adults. All of your buzz groups meet simultaneously in different parts of the room. If you have chairs in your room, encour-

age each group to bring their chairs together to facilitate discussion. If you are meeting in a room with pews, you may have to ask each group to get together in a different part of the room and have some of them turn around in the pew so they can talk more easily with those behind them. Assign each group a separate topic or a different facet of a topic. Ask each one then to select a leader who will guide their discussion and a secretary to write down their findings and be ready to report on them later. An example of the use of this method appears in the sample lesson plan in APPENDIX C. At a given signal, the entire group should reconvene, and leaders share the findings of their respective groups.

A variation of the Buzz group is a Three-some. Using this model, you would divide your adults into groups of three's, and assign each individual in each group one of these numbers: 1, 2, or 3. Each group would then follow this format in their discussion of a particular topic being dealt with at the time. For example, they are studying I John 5, and you come to verses 16 and 17, where the "sin unto death" is mentioned. Person #1 starts by sharing his opinion and ideas on the meaning of this sin with Person #2. Maximum time allowed would be two minutes. Person #2 may then ask Person #3 any question he wishes about what was said by Person #1. Person #3 tries to answer that question within two minutes. When all the groups have finished their discussions, reconvene the class and call on each Three-some to repeat the question they raised and their answer to it. Using this method may at first seem a little awkward, but it has some advantages:

a. All of those in a group get involved; no one can just sit back and let the more talkative ones dominate the conversation.
b. They get to know each other better. If you use this method again, be sure to reassign members to different groups.
c. They have to listen carefully to the conversation in order to respond intelligently, a key factor sometimes missing in a regular discussion.

If you use either of these models, you may find it beneficial at the conclusion of the discussions to enlist one adult from each group to record on your dry erase board some of the key thoughts or principles discovered by that group. You could then use these notes on the board at the end of this session to summarize their findings and make some applications.

y. This method is no newcomer to the educational scene. e suggested that it dates back as far as Plato or Aristotle. ou describe a problem situation (real or hypothetical) in which an individual is faced with a crisis that demands a decision or course of action. For example, Debbie is a dedicated Christian wife, trying to keep her testimony as she copes with Max, an unsaved husband, who is an alcoholic. One night after dinner, he announces to Debbie that he is going down to the local bar for a drink and wants her to go with him. Furthermore, he threatens her with the fact that if she doesn't go with him, he will find a woman who will. Guide your adults into a discussion of possible options for Debbie in this situation, particularly in the light of Ephesians 5:22, "Wives, submit yourselves unto your own husbands, as unto the Lord." You may well have some Christian women present who are struggling with similar problems, so try to draw some Biblically based conclusions that will be helpful to them.

6. Circle Response. If your group is not too large, arrange for the members to be seated in a circle. If it is too much trouble to move the chairs, simply start the discussion with the individual at the left end of the first row, go down that row, then down the next row, etc. until you reach the last individual on one end of the back row. Announce a question or a problem to the group. For example, "Is it a sin for a Christian to get angry?" Ask volunteers to read the following passages: James 1:19, 20; Ephesians 4:31; Colossians 3:8; Matthew 5:22; Mark 3:5. Seek to answer this question in the light of these verses. If the class is seated in a circle, ask one person to begin the discussion by offering a possible answer to this question. Then the next person on the right comments on the original question or upon the views of any who have already spoken. Everyone is to speak only once and in turn. Be sure to preface the discussion by informing your adults that those who do not wish to participate may simply say, "I pass" when their turn comes to speak. Again, when everyone has spoken, be sure to draw some Scripturally based conclusions in answering this discussion.

A variation of this method would be, after getting your adults seated in the circle, to distribute 3x5 cards to them. Ask a question that would stretch their minds, such as "If you could change one thing about your life right now, what would it be?" Give class members sufficient time to write their response on the cards, and then go around the circle, asking them to share their answers.

By the way, there is a neat fringe benefit to using this method. Years ago I was teaching a College and Career Sunday School class, and I noted that one of the young men in the back corner of the room was slipping in and out of "the Twilight Zone." So when I told them we were going to use this method as we dealt with a certain problem or question, I planned it so this guy was the very last person to speak to this issue. Results? He had to stay awake, because he knew he was the last one to speak and would need to stay alert to hear what everyone had said before him. Devious? Definitely, but it worked. What can I say? I'm an incurable pragmatist!

7. Couple Buzzers. Sometime referred to as "Neighbor Nudge," this is a modification of the Buzz group method, which you could use if you wanted to get all your adults involved quickly, without going through the hassle of moving your chairs. In this method, you would divide members into couples rather than groups. For example, your lesson topic is the Christian and money, and you want to deal with the pros and cons for using credit cards. Ask your adults to select one of the persons on either side of them and talk about this issue. Encourage each couple to make two lists: the pros (arguments for using credit cards) and the cons (arguments for not using them). After a brief time of discussion (the more individuals you have present, the less time you can allow for this) call the group back together. You might want to ask first for the pros and allow individuals to list their ideas. Then call for the cons. Try to draw some Biblically based conclusions concerning this issue.

8. Demonstration. Show your adults how to perform a certain task. You may wish to enlist one or more of them to help you in the demonstration. For example, if you are teaching a class on personal evangelism, you might call on one of your members to be the "unsaved" individual, and then show your class how you would lead that person to the Lord. And don't forget to show them also how to begin follow-up and discipleship of a new believer. Sadly, in too many instances we haven't done a very good job in this area.

9. Discussion. In this method, you get the ball rolling by asking a provoc-

ative, stimulating question. For example, in your lesson you are studying I Timothy 5, and you come to verse 23, "Drink no longer water, but use a little wine for thy stomach's sake and thine often infirmities." Since some believers today apparently have no problem with drinking wine, you might want to throw out the question, "Does the Bible teach total abstinence?" Warning: you could be opening a real "can of worms." In fact, you could be unleashing a "weapon of mass destruction!" Now certainly not every question you might wish to introduce for a discussion has to be this controversial, but for any discussion to be productive, you will need to follow some simple guidelines:

a. Encourage interaction and exchange of opinions among your adults, not just interaction with you, but also interaction with one another. Caution: if you encourage this type of dialogue, keep your eye on "the temperature gauge." If you detect disagreement between individuals that is leading to heated exchanges and a rise in the hostility level, you may need to step in and lead the discussion to "a cooler climate."

b. Don't allow certain individuals to dominate the discussion or start preaching mini-sermons. If you detect this beginning to happen, thank them for mentioning a particular point and then move on. To keep these adults controlled, you may need to bypass them and begin calling on others for their ideas and contributions. If all else fails, you may need to approach these offenders outside the class and kindly ask them for their cooperation in allowing others to participate. This particular problem seems to become more acute if you are the student paying big bucks for this instruction, such as is offered in an undergraduate or graduate course. One of the most frustrating experiences of my graduate studies was being in a class where one of my classmates felt compelled to dominate the time with his periodic spiritual filibusters. If you have ever been in a similar situation, you may have found yourself searching your brain for some painless (and sinless) way to shut this guy up, such as stuffing a sock in his mouth.

c. Don't let anyone lead a group "down rabbit trails" that provide little, if any, meaningful contribution to the topic being addressed.

d. Don't intentionally get a group involved in an issue that you don't have enough time nor knowledge to deal with adequately. One country preacher put it into perspective when he said,

"Don't uncover more snakes than you have time to kill."
e. Most importantly, as in all of these methods, be sure to summarize the contributions of your adults and articulate some specific conclusions.

10. Interview. Invite into your class or group a resource person who has enough expertise to speak with some authority to a particular issue, and interview this individual before the group. Options in using this method could include the following:

   a. After selecting a topic, invite your adults to submit questions they would like answered. Enlist your resource person and provide that individual with a copy of these questions. This person would then come to your class, be introduced, and proceed to field your members' questions, either from their list, or any related to it.
   b. Ask your resource person to address the issue in a lecture, and then follow that lecture by opening the floor for questions from the group.
   c. Invite in your resource person, and then you as the teacher ask questions from a prepared list, at the same time welcoming any additional questions from your members.

   Possible topics for such interviews could include the AIDS crisis, the creation-evolution debate, and the Bible and archaeology. This list would be limited only by your creativity and ability to find resource persons. Incidentally, it might be a good idea, sometime during the week preceding the lesson, to send your resource person a brief reminder of the commitment to meet with your group; and after the meeting, be sure to send a "thank you" note.

11. Lecture. In this method, you do most, if not all, of the talking using a prepared outline or notes. For example, you present a well-outlined thirty-minute lecture dealing with a doctrine, such as Sanctification or a Scripture passage, such as Matthew 4:1-11, which recounts the temptation of Christ in the wilderness. From my observation, limited as it may be, the lecture seems to be the method of choice among Christians who teach adults, whether they are in Sunday school or graduate school. Stick your head in one of these classes, and more than likely you note that the teacher is talking, and the members are listening (or giving that impression). There is little, if any, inter-

change of ideas between the teacher and the class. Frankly, this concerns me. For I am convinced that the straight lecture (defined here as the method where you as the teacher do all the talking) is not the most productive procedure to use in helping your adults to learn.

For this reason, I would like to spend more time on this method than I will on the others. But to be fair, let me first list some of the advantages in using the lecture.

a. It is, relatively speaking, easier to prepare. While you will surely be investing considerable time in studying, you will not have to worry about preparing slides for a PowerPoint presentation or transparencies for an overhead projector.
b. It is easier to present. You don't have problems fumbling with a burned out bulb in an overhead projector or a laptop that suddenly becomes "carnal" and refuses to obey your commands. After seeing this happen so many times to preachers and teachers, I have been tempted to believe that the Devil has assigned a special corps of demons to invade Christians' laptops and projectors causing them to malfunction either before or during a very important presentation!
c. It enables you to present your material in a well-organized way.
d. It enables you as the teacher to maintain better control of your teaching situation. In fact, I heard about one individual who made it obvious that he did not welcome any student feedback during his classes. And then there was another teacher who, when a student raised his hand to ask a question, said something like this, "I don't have time for your questions; I have to cover this material."
e. It enables you to present the most information in your allotted time.
f. It can be used with just about any number of students, from 5 to 5,000.
g. It allows you to share, in a relatively short time span, materials that may have taken months and years to accumulate, along with materials that may be difficult or impossible to locate today.

Wow! That's a pretty impressive list of advantages. I can almost hear some reader asking me, "What is your problem anyway?" Well, my "problem" with the straight lecture is best illustrated in the following list of its disadvantages.

a. It may confuse you by thinking that because you have talked, you have taught. As I pointed out with Match #6, if you define teaching as helping your adults change their behavior, then these two terms are not necessarily synonymous. While it is true that many times teaching will involve talking, it is nevertheless possible, as we observed earlier, that you can talk for thirty minutes and teach little, if anything, to your adults. This is probably my most serious criticism of the lecture.
b. If used by itself, it has a poor track record in helping adults retain the information you share with them. Studies done some years ago, indicated that students retain only 10 percent of what they hear, but that they retain 90 percent of what they see, hear, and do.
c. It provides little, if any, opportunity for your adults to get involved in your lesson. More about that one later.
d. It provides little, if any, opportunity for you to receive feedback from your adults. If they don't understand what you are saying, most of them will never let you know it.
e. It may gain your adults' attention initially, but it will probably lose them soon. You see, there's nothing terribly exciting about watching a "talking head" for thirty minutes. Incidentally, I feel that this type of presentation is a serious flaw in many of the videos that are professionally prepared for Christian educational purposes.
f. Unless your audience has paid some big bucks to hear you and receive a big notebook as part of that price, and unless you are an exceptionally, great communicator (demonstrating variety in your speaking voice, and having excellent content, sprinkled with appropriate illustrations and humor), you may become B-O-R-I-N-G very quickly and send the best of saints into a semi-comatose state! In fact, the lecture has been facetiously defined as "talking in somebody else's sleep." Someone else referred to it as "the process whereby the notes of the instructor get to the notes of the student, without passing through the minds of either." I am reminded of an incident that happened in one of my classes some time ago. It seems that we were talking about the lecture method, and I asked the class for their evaluation of it. One guy promptly responded, "I ain't big on it." And reflecting back on the list of disadvantages of the straight lecture, I confess I must agree with

that student. "I ain't big on it."

Summarily, if you have been using the lecture method for the past 50 years, I have no delusions that what I have just said is going to cause you suddenly to change your teaching strategy. But if you do choose to continue to use the lecture, you will probably find that you can maximize its effectiveness by using it in conjunction with audio-visuals and other methods that get your adults involved such as questions, role plays, buzz groups, etc.

12. Open-ended story. In this method, sometimes referred to as an unfinished story, you would describe a real or hypothetical scenario (a variation of the case study). Continue the story to a point where a problem develops that requires the key character to make a decision. The individual is faced with the options of making Choice A, which is supported by Scriptural principles but may generate problems for the character and/or others in the story; or Choice B, which is in violation of Scriptural principles but reduces or eliminates those problems. Let me give you an example. Let's say, Sue is a Christian, who works for Lee, an unsaved trial lawyer. One morning, Lee rushes into the office, with his attache case in one hand and a stack of folders in the other. As he passes by Sue's desk on his way to his office he says, "I have got a ton of stuff to get ready for that Davis trial at 2:00 this afternoon. If anyone calls, tell them I'm not here." Sue now has a problem. She can lie, grieve the Spirit, but keep her boss happy, OR she can tell the truth, please the Lord, but make her boss very unhappy. At that point, terminate the story, and ask your adults to discuss Sue's dilemma and come up with a course of action she should take. Encourage them to be candid and honest in their suggestions.

A variation of this method would be to distribute copies of your story to the individuals you have present. Include details right up to the climax, which calls for Sue to make a decision. Leave the rest of the story unfinished and ask your adults to write out how they would handle this situation. When everyone is finished, ask different class members to read their ending to the story.

Another variation would be to assign the roles of the characters who appear in the story to members of your group, selecting someone to play the role of Lee and someone to play the part of Sue. Discuss the scenario briefly with both individuals and tape them with your cam-

corder as they act out their parts. When they come to the clima
calls for Sue to make a decision, stop the recording. Later, eithe
day, or in the near future, play that tape for your adults, stop it at the
point of Sue's decision, and then ask them for their suggestions as to
how she should handle this situation. One of the advantages of taping
the role play is that you could save it for use in another teaching situation. With a little bit of "sanctified imagination," you will probably
think of other modifications of this method to use.

13. Question. This was one of Jesus' favorite methods, and you would
    do well to include it in your repertoire of teaching strategies. Here is
    a list of suggestions that I hope will enable you to use questions more
    effectively.

    a. Be sure your adults understand your question. If they don't, one
       of two things will usually happen.
       (1) They will hesitate to respond, or perhaps not respond at all,
           for fear of appearing to be brain-dead.
       (2) They will give you the wrong answer. Recently I came
           across a classic example of this. A public school teacher asked
           her students, "In what was the Declaration of Independence
           written?" The answer she was looking for was the specific
           year. The answer she received was, "in ink." This illustration
           reminds me of the small boy's reply when he was criticized
           for his answer to a teacher's question. He defended himself by
           simply saying, "Dumb question, dumb answer."

    b. Plan your questions beforehand and write (or type) them in
       your lesson plan. Writing them out will not only remind you to
       ask them but also help you periodically to finely tune them for
       clarity. Of course, even if you write out your questions, don't
       read them to your adults. Look into their faces when you ask a
       question and continue to look at them while you wait for their
       response. Be alert to modify your questions, if necessary, and ask
       any impromptu ones that would be relevant to your discussion.

    c. Sometimes you will want to throw out a question to the entire
       group. At other times, you might want to ask the question, pause
       (to get everyone's attention), and then call on a particular individual to reply. Never use this tactic intentionally to embarrass
       an adult.

d. Ask rhetorical questions. These are not intended to call for any type of response from your adults (explain this to them before you ask the question), but this type can be used to call for some serious, personal inventory of their lives. Examples: "When is the last time we (probably be better if you include yourself in this equation) wept over an unsaved loved one or neighbor?" "When is the last time we handed out a tract or tried to lead someone to Christ?" "How much time did we spend today with the Lord in His Word and prayer?"

e. Encourage your adults to ask questions. Actually, you should probably be concerned if they have no questions. Occasionally, during your lesson, just stop and ask something such as, "Any questions?" And this brings us to an interesting thought. What do you do if they ask you a question, and you don't know the answer? At this point, you have several options

(1) Ask for prayer requests
(2) Call for some testimonies
(3) Dismiss class early
(4) None of the above

If you picked option (4), congratulations! Seriously, if you don't know the answer to their question, simply admit it, but promise that you will do some research to find it and bring it back with you the next time you meet with them. And if you make that promise, be sure to keep it. Even then, you may be looking for the answer to a question that has baffled theologians for centuries, but give it your best shot. Just remember, being ignorant in some instances may not be a disgrace, but remaining ignorant is.

f. Occasionally turn an individual's question back to the others present and ask for their comments. CAUTION: never use this procedure to cover up the fact that you don't know the answer. If you do, and poll your adults on their thoughts concerning the question, almost invariably someone is eventually going to throw it right back into your lap and ask, "Teacher, what do you think?" Instant sweat time! It's far better (and a bit more honest) to simply admit you don't know the answer and follow the procedure given in the previous point.

g. After asking the question, give your listeners some time to think. Don't get impatient if there is no immediate response and answer the question yourself. If you are continually answering your own questions, this method is going to lose some of its edge in getting their attention. If there is some delay in the responses to your question, you might suggest, "O.K., let's take a minute to think about this one."

h. Try to avoid questions that call for a simple "yes" or "no" answer. I think it is better to ask questions that tend to stretch minds and provoke some serious thinking. To me, the question "Is Jesus God?" is not nearly as effective as "Why do you believe Jesus is God?" Here's another example. Rather than asking them, "What does the Bible say about us loving our enemies?" pose the question, "What should I do when my neighbor's Lab puppy gets out during the day and destroys my prize rose bush?"

i. Avoid asking questions which you are reasonably sure that they (nor anyone else on planet earth) can answer. Extreme examples?

   (1) When Adam sinned, what time of day was it?
   (2) Will a man in his resurrected body get all his fingernail clippings back?
   (3) Do angels shine brighter in the morning than in the evening?

   I think I can hear someone say right about now, "You have to be kidding. Who would ever ask stupid questions like these?" Well, theologians during the Scholastic Period, who didn't have computers or video games to keep them occupied, did actually debate issues like these. I wouldn't recommend that you go there.

j. Ask only one question at a time. Most of us have seen interviews or press conferences in which someone in the audience has posed a question with two or three parts, the answer of each generally contingent upon the answer of the former. Personally, my limited I.Q. makes me stand in awe of the person who is able to navigate these types of questions sequentially and come up with the correct answers to all the components.

k. Occasionally direct questions to shy or non-participating adults, again taking care not to embarrass them. Incidentally, what do you do about that fellow who has slipped into a coma in the third row? I confess that in the past I have been seriously tempted to ask him a question in order to resuscitate him, but my reluctance to cause additional embarrassment has put the brakes on this idea. Actually, I may be part of his problem. In that connection, I'm reminded of the story of the preacher who had a man fall asleep during his sermon. He called out to a man sitting next to the slumbering brother, "Hey, wake him up!" Without missing a beat, the man responded, "You wake him up. You put him to sleep."

l. Avoid repeating questions. If your adults are reasonably sure you are always going to ask your questions twice, they just might just decide to wait for the second time around.

14. Research project. In this method you are asking your adults to research a project and bring back to the group their findings. In an academic setting, this usually takes the form of projects and term papers, but this method can also be useful in the adult Sunday school class, where it can have a number of variations.

    a. Ask one adult to prepare a report, for example, on Herod's temple, and later share it at some point in your lesson.
    b. Ask class members to interview individuals and relate their findings to the class. As an illustration, you could ask some of your members to visit some of the shut-ins of your church and ask them what the church can do to minister to their needs. Bring back this report and share it with your class. Years ago in one of our youth leadership classes, I assigned to the students a project, which may not be exactly appropriate for your class. I asked them to go out and interview at least one individual who had been on drugs and ask, among other things, the reason why that person had begun taking drugs. If the individual consented, our student was to tape this interview, bring it back to our class, and play it for us. As we listened that day to those tapes, it was both ironic and sad that a recurring reason given for their substance abuse was that it made them feel important.
    c. Ask one of your more mature (and willing) adults to teach a section of your lesson on a certain Sunday. I gleaned this idea from a missionary friend who had served the Lord for almost thirty years in Bolivia and had experienced a very effective teaching ministry there. She shared with me that she used this approach sometimes once a month and would eventually invite each member in her group to participate. This strategy, she reported, not only helped her gain and sustain attention in the class but also enabled her to discover any individuals who demonstrated

the gift of teaching. If you used this method, you would want to encourage such individuals to take further instruction and look for opportunities to use that gift.

15. Role Play. This method can be very effective, but I would like to defer my comments about it until we put a slightly different spin on it with Match #17

16. Skit. Unlike the Role Play, with this method you select two or more of your adults to prepare and present a rehearsed enactment of a real or hypothetical situation. Example: years ago, we wanted to present in our Sunday school staff meeting a skit on how not to visit a Sunday school student in his home. We needed four individuals to act the parts of the child, his mom and dad, and the Sunday school teacher. Fortunately, one of our church members had some experience in acting, along with a fantastic sense of humor. We asked her to be the teacher making the visit. The four practiced with a script, and on the night of their presentation, my only regret is that I was unable to videotape it. The antics of our "teacher" not only kept us laughing but also powerfully impacted us concerning the importance of teachers visiting their students, and how not to do it.

A bit of prayerful creativity should generate a number of possibilities for using skits in your teaching. Examples might include the following: How not to witness to a friend, or How not to visit a friend in the hospital. At the conclusion of the skit, take a few moments to express your appreciation for the work of the actors and actresses, and discuss with your class the implications of the skit's message for their lives.

17. Teacher-student dialogue. In this method, you select one adult in your group and conduct a conversation with that individual while the others listen. Again, you must be extremely careful that you do not embarrass the person, but generally, you should be able to recruit someone who will go along with this plan. Let me give you an example how this could work. In your lesson you are studying the Sermon on the Mount and come to Matthew 5:13 where Jesus said, "Ye are the salt of the earth." While the rest of the group listens, call on the adult you have selected and ask that person a series of questions, such as:

   a. "What are some of the ways in which we use salt today?"

b. "What does Jesus mean here when He refers to believers as the salt of the earth?"
c. "How can we as believers become salt in our culture?"

It is important that you allocate sufficient time to wait for the person's responses to each question, discuss them, summarize conclusions, and make applications if possible. I have usually found this effective in sustaining the attention, not just of the person being questioned, but also the rest of the adults who are listening.

DEFINITELY QUOTABLE:

"A rut is a grave with the ends knocked out." Laurence J. Peter
"Choose your rut carefully. You'll be in it for the next 150 miles." A sign along an Alaskan highway.

STRIKE THE MATCH:

If you feel that maybe you have been in a "rut" recently in your teaching, using the same methods repeatedly, why not look over the list above, see if you can find one that would be appropriate to your next lesson, bathe it in prayer, and use it. I believe that you (and your adults) will enjoy doing something new if it proves to be effective in the learning process.

MATCH

17

OCCASIONALLY ASSIGN NAMES OF YOUR ADULTS TO THE CHARACTERS YOU USE IN A ROLE PLAY OR CASE STUDY

Since I merely mentioned the role play in the list of methods discussed under the preceding "Match," and some of you may not be familiar with it, let me explain briefly how it works. This is an unrehearsed form of drama, in which you select 2-5 adults to participate. A couple of quick cautions:

1. Don't select adults who are shy introverts, but if possible, pick the extroverts, especially those who may have a flair for the dramatic.
2. Don't choose adults who may be currently struggling with the same type of situation you are going to ask them to portray. To illustrate, if you are teaching middle-aged adults, some of whom still have teens at home, and you want to structure a role play which pictures some Christian parents seeking to deal with a rebellious teen, it could be potentially embarrassing to select adults to play those parts, if they are currently facing a similar crisis at home.

Once you have selected your adults, you may wish to assign them fictitious names. Personally, I have found it to be more effective in gaining and sustaining class attention if I allow the adults chosen to keep their own names during the role play. Next, you should describe an actual or hypothetical situation, ask the adults to assume the roles of the chief characters in the story, and then "turn them loose" to play out the situation in the manner they feel their roles require. O.K., let's "test drive" this method and show you how it might play.

You are teaching a Sunday school class of young marrieds. This Sunday morning you want to help your adults learn how to make a visit in the home of some new neighbors, looking for the opportunity to invite them to your church and maybe even share a personal witness with them. You need two couples in this scenario, so you choose Gene and Claudia (husband and wife) to play the part of the Christians making the visit and Tom and Dot (husband and wife) to play the part of their new, unsaved neighbors. Then you arrange at the front of the room four chairs to represent the living room of Tom and Dot and ask them to take two of the seats. Ask Gene and Claudia to stand to one side of the room. Your instructions to the couples might run something like this: "Tom and Dot, you are both unsaved, but once attended church fairly regularly in the small town where you used to live. Then one day the pastor of that church had an affair with the church secretary and deserted his wife and three small children. As a result, you are convinced that the church is full of hypocrites, and want nothing to do with it or Christianity. Now obviously, Gene and Claudia, you know nothing of this situation, but one night on church visitation, you show up at Tom and Dot's door and ring the bell." At that point, you simply turn the action over to your actors to play out this situation any way they feel appropriate. Length of time allowed for this method will generally range from two to ten minutes. When you feel enough time has elapsed to demonstrate your point, interrupt the action, and ask the actors and the rest of the class to evaluate the behavior of the characters portrayed in the role play. For example, ask either one individual or the entire group, "How do feel about the way Claudia responded to Dot's objections?" After allowing time for discussion, draw some conclusions, and share any lessons we need to learn from this role play. Be sure to express your appreciation to the two couples for their participation.

A slight modification of the role play is "playing the devil's advocate." Let me illustrate how this one would work. You are teaching a Sunday school class of middle aged adults. Select Harry, whom you know is a faithful witness for the Lord, to play the role of a Christian seeking to win you to Christ. To make this just a bit more challenging for him, you play the role of a devout, unsaved Roman Catholic, steeped for years in the doctrinal heresy of this system. Obviously, to make this work, you will need to brush up on some of the basic teachings of the Catholic church, so you can periodically raise objections to his witness because of what you have been previously taught. For example, when he says you need to receive Christ, you, as a faithful Catholic, might reply, "But I do this every time I accept the wafer from my priest." After enough time has elapsed to demonstrate his ability to deal with you, stop the action, and ask your class to evaluate Harry's handling of this situation. Seek to emphasize the lessons class members need to learn if they ever hope to be effective in their witnessing to Catholics. When you are finished, be sure to thank Harry for his willingness to participate.

As the title of this section suggests, this strategy of allowing your adults to retain their own names could also work well when using a case study (this method already discussed with Match #16). Let me suggest here an illustration. You are dealing in your lesson with Jehovah Witnesses, including some of their doctrinal heresies and guidelines for witnessing to them. Select Wanda, one of the adult women in your group, and present the following scenario: "Wanda, at work you have been getting acquainted with Louise, another employee in the office. You have been going on coffee break with her for the past week, and you don't believe she is a Christian, so you are praying for the right opportunity to give at least a brief witness to her on one of your breaks. Well, today seems to be the right time, so while you both are drinking your coffee and making small talk, you manage to steer the conversation to the question of her salvation. She listens very politely while you share the Gospel with her, eventually mentioning that because God loved us so much, He sent His own Son Jesus to die on the cross for our sins and be raised again to save all who would come to Him. At this point, Louise breaks the news to you that she is a member of the Jehovah's Witnesses and that she believes Jesus was simply a created being, Michael the Archangel, to be exact, and that when He died on the cross, He remained dead and was never resurrected. Wanda, how would you handle this situation?" After you have allowed sufficient time for her to respond, you may want to open the discussion to the rest of those present, who can take turns addressing this issue.

Summarily, I am convinced that both the role play and case study

e very powerful tools for you to use in your teaching.
the scenarios discussed above, they seem to be particularly
when training your adults to become more effective in their
d soul winning.

DEFINITELY QUOTABLE:

"The Good News of the Gospel is Good News only if it reaches the lost before it's too late."

"Soul-winning is house-hunting for God." See I Corinthians 6:19, 20.

STRIKE THE MATCH

Read over this "Match" again to familiarize yourself with how it works and try it soon with your class. I believe you will like the results.

MATCH 18

GET YOUR ADULTS INVOLVED IN THE LESSON

I remember the day very well. I had been asked to substitute for a teacher in an older adult Sunday school class. Since I knew the teacher and was aware that he used the lecture method fairly regularly, I thought it would be a good idea to introduce the class to buzz groups. I planned to use three groups, select a leader for each, and distribute a set of prepared handouts that contained an assignment for each group. Inasmuch as the chairs in that room had been arranged the same way for the past 300 years, all very neatly placed in rows facing the front, we felt it might be a good idea to introduce some variety in that department too. So we arrived early that morning, and with the help of some of the men, proceeded to place the chairs in three circles and await the members' arrival. Well, they soon began to trickle in, and their responses to their new environment were indeed a "mixed bag." Most of the class members seemed very interested and wanted to know what this was all about. Some arrived, took one look at this new situation, and decided they wanted absolutely nothing to do with it. Pulling some other chairs to the back of the room, they camped there for the entire class session. From some of their looks and remarks, I had the eerie sensation that I was doing something very heretical, perilously similar to denying the Trinity! Well, after several attempts to allay their fears by reminding them I merely wanted them to "think outside the box" for a brief time, we explained the game plan to the group, and encouraged them to participate. In retrospect, judging from their enthusiasm, level of participation, and responses, I feel that this was a very profitable session. They seemed to enjoy this opportunity to be involved in the class.

From that experience and many others, I have concluded that most adults will welcome that same opportunity. In fact, I have seen adults, when not given the opportunity to be involved, actually interrupt the teacher with their questions. For far too long, Christian teachers have been teaching adults with the premise that all those adults want to do in class is "Sit, Soak, and Sour." We must change this mentality. When you teach a child to swim, you don't sit him down and lecture to him for thirty minutes on the theory of buoyance and proper leg flexion. No, he learns to swim by being involved in the water. In similar fashion, adults learn by being involved in the process of teaching. In fact, I read of a church that had a policy that you could not teach their adults if you did not share their vision of actively involving their adult learners in the classroom. Assuming that you agree with this concept of involving them, the big question now becomes how? Here are a few simple suggestions:

1. Inform them up front that you will genuinely welcome their interaction with you and their fellow class mates. Work on developing an atmosphere of spontaneity.
2. Encourage them to question you concerning any point that they may not understand. But do this throughout the lesson. Don't wait until the last two minutes of your class. By that time, most of them will probably be too numb to care.
3. Use a variety of teaching methods that will get them involved. Look back over the list given you with Match #16. The ones that have worked particularly well for me in this area are Buzz Groups, discussion, brainstorming, questions, and circle response.
4. Sometimes when an adult asks you a question, rather than giving the answer, throw it back to the others with your question, "What do you think?"
5. Prepare and distribute handouts, perhaps with the main points of your outline, and leave blank spaces where your adults can write in the information as you present it during the lesson. This gets them involved, helps maintain their attention, and keeps them aware of the progress you are making in covering the material. If you are exceptionally boring that day, your outline may also give them hope that you will soon be finished.
6. If the topic of your lesson is appropriate, prepare a 3x5 card for each

member of your class. On a third of the cards type these words: "How I was saved." On another third, type the words: "A great answer to prayer." On the final third, put the words: "A time when God did the impossible." Distribute these cards to your class members and ask them to write in the information requested. After about five minutes, ask them to share their answers with the rest of the class.

Now having given you this sales pitch on involving adults, let me give you the bad news. Let's face it. If you teach long enough, you will meet some adults who suffer from that disorder which I would term the "Sphinx Syndrome" (a fairly common malady among adults that seems to become more severe with age). They just sit there in silence. They do not answer any of your questions. They do not get involved in any of your class discussions. They do not participate, period. Now, there could be a number of reasons for this, and that list will probably include one or more of the following:

1. Serious spiritual need - unsaved or carnal
2. Difficulty in hearing
3. Dislike for you and/or your teaching
4. Reluctance to attempt anything new that will bump them out of their "comfort zone"
5. Shyness

While I have at one time or another, had to deal with all of these, let me focus on numbers 4 and 5, which could be related. If you are currently faced with these problems, let me suggest a simple plan of sequential steps that you may find helpful in getting these individuals increasingly involved in your lesson.

1. First, use a very non-threatening procedure, such as asking each adult to read silently a certain Scripture passage and look for a truth or answer a question. For example, if this next lesson is on Matthew 4:1-11, ask your group to read over this passage and discover the weapon that Jesus used to overcome Satan's temptations in the wilderness. Later, you can ask them to share their findings, and though your shy adults probably won't even breathe deeply for fear of being recognized, you did succeed in getting them, to some extent, involved in the lesson.

2. If you can notice some success with this first procedure, you might want to move on to the next step, a method called Couple Buzzers, referred to by some Christian educators as Neighbor Nudge. With Match #16, we looked at a definition of this method with an illustration how you could use it in your teaching. The objective is to get your adults to extend their involvement to just one other individual during the lesson. It has been my experience that this procedure usually gets even the most shy adults participating.

3. Now, if you notice that these first two steps are working, you may want to get a little bolder and move on to the third step, Buzz Groups. A definition of this method was also given with Match #16. If possible, keep the size of each group reasonably small, perhaps a maximum of 5-6 members. This will make it possible for more adults to participate, especially those shy ones, who would not think of expressing their opinions before everyone there, but might feel comfortable sharing their views within their small group.

4. A fourth step would be to seek their participation in methods involving the entire group, such as discussions, questions, and brainstorming. For example, your adults are studying James 2:8, and they are discussing the meaning of this verse. If you have watched Brad slowly overcome some of his shyness, you might gently seek his opinion, "Brad, what do you think?"

5. The final step (and being realistic, some of your adults will probably never reach this level) is to ask one individual to do something alone before the entire group, such as bring in a brief report and share it with the members. For example, in your next lesson you are supposed to deal with the trial and crucifixion of Jesus. If you can find a volunteer, ask for a 2-3 minute report on the life and work of Pilate. Although such an assignment would be scary to many adults, hopefully you will find someone who would be willing to tackle it. You might want to phone or e-mail this person early in the week to get a progress report on work being done and offer any assistance that may be needed. Later be sure to express your appreciation to this individual for the work done.

DEFINITELY QUOTABLE:

"Experience is a good teacher, but the tuition is expensive."

"The church is full of willing workers. Some are willing to work, and the rest are willing to watch them."

STRIKE THE MATCH:

If you are currently responsible for teaching a group of adults, and some of them suffer from the "Sphinx Syndrome," let me suggest that you review the five steps listed above at the end of this Match and seek to implement them in a future lesson.

MATCH

19

LOOK THEM IN THE EYE

He was the pastor of an evangelical church in the South. He seemed to be a solid Biblicist and a fairly good speaker, but when he preached, he usually kept his eyes focused on the balcony. The only problem was the church had no balcony! Seriously, most of the time he was not looking at his congregation, but for some unknown reason, seemed to be obsessed with the space above their heads. Now let's face it. Not all of us are that great to look at, but this quirk is, to say the least, a bit distractive. Unfortunately this pastor's problem is also shared by some teachers today. Rather than look at their students, their eyes appear to be focused on the back wall of the room (it is possible that they may be staring at the clock, silently praying for the passing of time). However, I believe strongly that one of the keys to being an effective teacher of adults is to maintain eye contact with them. And while most of us will need to glance down at our notes periodically to refresh our memories, just don't stay interred there. One of the surest ways to avoid this problem is to make adequate preparation for your lesson. If you have been faithful in doing this, you will not need to submerge yourself in your notes; you will have more time to look into the faces of your adults. Here are a few suggestions to keep in mind while you are teaching.

1. Periodically allow your eyes "to sweep" from one side of the room to the other. Then select one section and "sweep" from the front row to the back. If your group is small (10 or 15), try during your lesson to

look into the face of each individual for a couple of seconds. Don't stop talking during this time. Staring silently at people may make them very uncomfortable. Most of us have vivid memories of a parent or teacher using this strategy to signal us of impending judgment because of our misbehavior. If your group is large, trying to look at each one might be not only impractical, but also very difficult. However, you could still, during your lesson, select different individuals perhaps in the first few rows, and look into their faces for a couple of seconds.

2. Avoid getting "locked" into one side of your room. Recently I have noticed myself favoring one side of the classroom and addressing the students in that section, while practically neglecting to look at the other side. I have found that the only solution is to discipline myself to give equal time to both.

3. Occasionally select one individual, if possible walk over near where the person is sitting, look right into their eyes, and use a brief teacher-student dialog, while the rest of your group listens (we looked at this method with Match #16).

Well, we have talked about the how, but now we need to talk about the why. What's the big deal about this looking into the eyes of your adults while teaching them? I would like to suggest it is very important for at least three reasons:

1. It will help you as the teacher to gain and sustain their attention. It just seems that there is something about looking directly at a person that generally causes that individual to look back at you. You will note I said, "generally." No amount of looking (or even staring!) on your part is going to be much help if a person's eyes are already covered with a moist glaze, usually indicating that the brain, along with the body, is poised to slip into a semi-conscious state. To bring these people back to your lesson, you will probably need to do something spectacular, such as calling in the U.S. Marine Corps Band!

2. It will give you as the teacher a more personal touch with your adults, for it will seem, at least for a couple of seconds, that you are involving yourself one-on-one with them as individuals.

3. It will serve as an "early warning device" to alert you that you have a problem. If they don't have a clue as to what you are talking about, you will possibly get a frown or a look of puzzlement. If they disagree with you, you will probably get signals such as shaking the head "east and west," contortion of facial features, or even open hostility.

DEFINITELY QUOTABLE:

"My wife says I never listen to her. At least, I think that's what she said." Words on a T-shirt.
"Most people know how to say nothing, but few know when."

STRIKE THE MATCH

The next time you have an occasion to teach a group of adults make a special effort periodically to look into their eyes during your lesson.

MATCH

20

USE ILLUSTRATIONS THROUGHOUT YOUR LESSON

Years ago, Herman Horne wrote a book entitled Jesus, the Master Teacher. Certainly, as you walk with Jesus through the Gospels, it soon becomes apparent that He indeed was (is) the Master Craftsman at the skill of communication. Let me mention just four evidences of this.

1. He had something to say, and He said it with authority. This was surely the opinion of His listeners, as exemplified by that Capernaum crowd, who quickly recognized the difference between Jesus and the Scribes, their former teachers. And then there was the response of those officers sent by the Pharisees and priests to apprehend Jesus and bring Him in, who returned empty-handed with their only excuse, "Never man spake like this Man."

2. He was able to gain and keep the attention of His listeners, illustrated by His use of the subject of the new birth to "hook" Nicodemus. Then we see Him in the next chapter of John talk about water in a physical well to get the attention of a Samaritan woman, who desperately needed to drink from God's eternal well.

3. He chose a variety of teaching methods. He used the lecture on the mountain and by the Sea of Galilee. He used questions with both His

disciples and His enemies. He used a modification of the problem-solving method when He faced five thousand hungry people and confronted Philip with the dilemma, "Whence are we to buy bread, that these may eat?" He frequently was involved with His disciples in discussions where topics ranged from the ridiculous (ex. the disciples' stupid debate over which of them was the greatest) to the sublime (ex. His Second Coming).

4. He constantly used illustrations to drive home the truths of His message. These at times were verbal, such as parables. One of the more well known would probably be the sower and the seed, but one of my favorites is about the Pharisee who thought he was praying, but because of his self-righteousness, was only talking "with himself." But Jesus also liberally sprinkled His teaching with visual metaphors, demonstrating a certain truth by comparing it to some object familiar to His listeners, such as a door, the lilies of the field, or a mountain.

And since the title of this section has to do with illustrations, let's camp here for a little while. It is my firm conviction that just as Jesus felt it necessary to use them, we as teachers should also be incorporating them into our lessons. Let me list a few reasons why illustrations are important.

1. They help you gain and sustain the attention of your adults. Have you ever been listening to a preacher or teacher for what seems like a mini-eternity, and your mind meanders off to other parts of the universe to grapple with such critical issues as whether or not you double-bolted the back door, or what you will eat for lunch, fast food or Chinese? And then it happens. The speaker begins to tell an interesting story, and it's almost as if someone flipped a switch. People around you seem to stop squirming in their seats, shuffling papers, or even reading their Bibles as that story acts almost like a magnet, drawing you and the rest of the group back to the speaker and his message.

I believe you will find this will also work for you. Try to use a "mind-grabbing" illustration to introduce your lesson and then periodically insert others into your presentation to help bring back those wandering minds. Through the years I have used the overhead projector rather extensively in my classes, and when I click on the switch, students will look up in the direction of the machine to check out the information on the transparency. Sometimes just as an experiment, I will click on the machine, and students' heads will "pop" up all over the class to look toward the screen. This could probably qualify as a classic illustration of Pavlov's conditioning!

2. Second, illustrations help your students understand what you are saying. This is especially true of visuals. Years ago, we were listening to our pastor, in his morning message, trying to explain to us the two compartments of the Tabernacle and where the furniture in each was located. As I listened to his valiant effort to sketch for us a mental picture of the layout, it became apparent that he was having a struggle. I could not help but think if he had only used one of the beautiful transparencies of the Tabernacle available at that time, he could have instantly clarified this for all of us.

3. Third, illustrations help stir our emotions. Some stories, for example, can make your adults cry; others can make them laugh. If you are not careful, however, you can begin to think of illustrations as just a strategy for manipulating individuals and causing them to make "decisions." Unfortunately, decisions which are driven by an emotional "hiccup" don't survive very long in the fire of reality. Yet, God did design us with emotions, and we need to minister in our teaching to that part of the individual. An appropriate story, well told, can serve this purpose very effectively.

To me, one of the stories that does this best is the account of the writing of that beautiful hymn "It Is Well With My Soul." While there are variations in the details concerning the composition of this song, let me share just the highlights of the story as it appears in the book, "Al Smith's Treasury of Hymn Histories." In 1871 the great Chicago fire decimated the real estate holdings of Horatio Spafford, a well-known Christian attorney in that city. In November of 1873 since many of the schools in the area had not yet been rebuilt, Mr. Spafford decided that he would take his family to England where he could enroll his four daughters in an English academy. At the time of their departure, however, a business commitment made it necessary for him to send his wife and children on with the promise that he would come on a later ship. He never saw his daughters again, for the ship on which they and their mother were traveling later collided with another vessel and sank, carrying most of the passengers, including the four girls, to their deaths. Mrs. Spafford was rescued, and upon reaching England, she sent a cablegram to her husband with only two words: "Saved, alone." And though this news brought great sorrow and despair to his soul, Spafford, armed with the confidence that God would not forsake him during this tragedy, was able to sit down and pen the words of this beloved hymn, to which P.P. Bliss later composed the melody. Rarely can I hear that song without thinking of the story behind it. It is a story that not only provides me with the song's historical context, but also ministers to my emotions, evoking sympathy for that dear brother, seeking to cope with the loss of his four precious daughters. It also gives me the quiet assurance, that when the storms of life roll over me, I can say with Spafford, "It is well. It is well with my soul." Amen.

Well, I hope by now you are convinced of the importance of illustrations. If so, let's look at some of the types of illustrations we can use to make our teaching more effective. They are listed below, with a few comments, under two categories: verbal and visual.

1. Types of verbal illustrations
    a. Jokes (more about this when we look at the need for a sense of humor).
    b. Statistics. The problem with these is they are constantly going out of date. If you clip a statistic for use, be sure to write on it somewhere the date it was released. After some time, most of these statistics should probably be trashed unless they can be used to compare with more recent ones.
    c. Stories. Some of these have been around a long time, and it seems that the longer they are around, and the more individuals repeat them, the more the details of the stories keep changing. This is probably why some pastors and teachers only use stories and illustrations from their personal lives. I'm not sure I agree with that decision, but I can understand their reason for making it. By the way, if you do use illustrations from your personal life, don't be guilty of overkill. Hearing anecdotes from your adolescent years about growing up on the farm can be interesting the first time; but if in each lesson you resurrect those experiences, including the names of your grandpa, cousins, mule, and hound dog on that little farm, you may soon have some of your mem-

bers silently wishing you were back there.

d. Quotations. For years I have been collecting both serious and humorous ones to use in the ministry. Some of these have been a tremendous blessing, not only to my life, but also apparently to many of those with whom I have shared them. Let me just give you a few.

"If you see a Bible that is falling apart, it probably belongs to someone who isn't." (Vance Havner)

"Life is a very fragile gift from God."

"A short prayer will reach the Throne if you don't live too far away." (seen on an outdoor church sign)

"Dear Lord, help me so to live here on earth that I will have the least to regret in eternity."

"By yielding to temptation, one may lose in a moment what took him a lifetime to gain."

"One of the greatest proofs for the supernatural origin of Christianity is the fact that it has survived all these centuries in spite of its followers."

"Lord, where we are wrong, make us willing to change; where we are right, make us easy to live with." (Peter Marshall)

"God always gives His best to those who leave the choice with Him." (Jim Elliot)

"It is better not to sin than to sin and be forgiven."

"Our disappointments are God's appointments." (Edith Young)

"There are no accidents in a Christian's life; only incidents in His perfect plan for us."(One of our dearest friends said it this way, "When I got saved, I ran out of luck.")

"Eternity is that time when you will wish you had done things you are not doing now."

"God buries His workmen but carries on His work." (Charles Wesley)

"Talk is cheap because supply exceeds demand." (Debbie Meier)

"How many people are not Christians because you are one?"

"Worry is interest paid on trouble before it falls due." (W.R. Inge)

"There is only one thing better than going to Heaven or one thing worse than going to hell. It is taking someone with you."

I hope these will be useful to you. Just remember, when you do cite a quotation, try to identify its author and quote it correctly.

2. Types of visual illustrations (Obviously the size of your visual illus-

trations will be determined by the size of your group.)

   a. Simple stick figures drawn on a dry erase board (far superior to the old chalkboard, since you can use colored markers, without having to cope with all that chalk dust.)
   b. Diagrams
   c. Graphs. You probably have computer software that can generate the basic types of graphs: pie, bar, and line.
   d. Charts. For example, one of these could be used very effectively to trace the history of our English Bible.
   e. Maps. If you are discussing Israel's journey from Egypt to the Promised Land, find a map of that area of the world at that time (a topographical map, transparency, or a PowerPoint slide) and trace the trip on your map.
   f. Object lessons. For example, bring in an oil lamp, light it, and ask your adults to discuss the question, "Why would Jesus refer to us as the light of the world?"
   g. Models. I have a friend who has constructed a beautiful scale model of Noah's Ark and uses it to lecture on the universal flood. As a young pastor, I was able to purchase a kit to build a scale model of the OT tabernacle and use it when teaching our adults.
   h. Overhead transparencies. Professionally prepared ones may be purchased, or you can use your computer to generate your own. It is definitely not the purpose of this section to give extensive instructions on the use of the overhead projector, but if you do use one, don't leave it on for the entire lesson. Turn it on when you refer to the information on the screen and then turn it off. This will not only extend the life of your machine's bulb but also, and more importantly, it will help you sustain the attention of your listeners.
   i. PowerPoint. This is a software program developed by Microsoft. Its primary purpose is to generate an audio-visual presentation of information using a computer. The image produced may be shown on the computer's screen or on a larger external screen by means of a multi-media projector. Because of its tremendous potential as a teaching tool, PowerPoint is rapidly becoming the method of choice among many educators.
   j. Videos or DVD's. These can be particularly effective as instructional tools. For example, show one to your parents on the

subject of rearing teenagers. My favorite one-liner on this subject was seen on the wall of a family restaurant and which read, "Mothers of teens know why some animals eat their young."

k. Dramatics. Role plays and skits were discussed earlier, but let me mention one more, the monologue. In this method, you stand or sit alone before your group and speak either to yourself, as musing, or to an imaginary audience who would be contemporary with the character you are assuming. Years ago, a pastor friend of mine surprised his Sunday morning congregation "big time" by coming to the pulpit dressed as the rich man of Luke 16. Wearing a costume, complete with chains, his sermon consisted of a monologue, in which the rich man bewailed his folly in failing to prepare to meet God and pleaded with Heaven to send Lazarus to warn his five brethren. Although I would not recommend doing a lot of this in lieu of a message, it seems that this pastor's dramatic presentation made a powerful impact on his congregation that Sunday.

DEFINITELY QUOTABLE:

"Clay has a lot of potential . . . but only in the hands of the Potter."
"Practice does not make perfect; practice makes permanent. Only perfect practice makes perfect." Vince Lombardi

STRIKE THE MATCH:

If you have not been accustomed to doing so, plan to use some verbal and visual illustrations the next time you teach, one as an introduction of your lesson and several more scattered throughout it. For those of you who already are using them in your teaching, why not look over the lists given above, and try a different one?

MATCH 21

SCHEDULE SURGERY FOR THAT MONOTONE

Fully aware that what I am about to say is going to serve as incriminating evidence for my lack of either spirituality or intelligence (perhaps both), I nevertheless have a confession to make. One of the first places I look at in the morning newspaper is the comics section. While I never bother to read most of them, there are a few strips that provide me with some really funny cartoons, which I have been adding to my collection through the years. One of my current favorites is Kudzu, which usually chronicles the antics and sayings of a chubby little preacher named Will B. Dunn. In one strip the first panel shows a TV set with the preacher and a man who is evidently a guest on what appears to be a talk show. In that panel, the guest looks at the preacher and says, "It's a miracle, Preacher! You and your TV show healed my affliction!" In the second panel, you see the preacher, exuberantly responding to his guest, "Hallelujah! . . . A miracle cure! And what was your affliction, Brother?" In the third panel, the preacher's face registers disappointment as his guest responds with one word, "Insomnia." I love it! But there's another "cure for insomnia" out there, and it will put some people to sleep almost as fast as Sominex. Its name is monotone.

A monotone has been defined as a succession of syllables, words, or sentences in one unvaried, (monotonous) key or pitch. Some people sing in monotone. If an individual with this "talent" comes to try out for your choir, I suggest you recommend an alternative ministry, such as folding the church bulletins. And then there are some monotones that try to teach. I am thinking of a faithful Christian teacher who had a beautiful, melodic bass voice. Every Christmas he would be asked to sing a solo in Handel's Messiah, and his deeply bass voice made his ministry a work of art. But unfortunately that wonderful voice became the "kiss of death" to his ministry as a teacher, since he seldom varied his volume or rate of speaking, making him a textbook monotone. Results? His students found it tough to stay awake and get anything out of his classes. If you are wondering whether or not you have this same problem, ask a friend to evaluate your teaching voice. Better still, make an audio tape of one of your lessons and listen to it later. Warning. I heard about a preacher who taped one of his sermons and went to sleep listening to the playback! If you do have a problem in this area, you need to schedule surgery for that monotone ASAP. Here are a few ideas you might want to try.

1. Vary your volume. If there is a point in your lesson that needs special emphasis, get excited and turn up your volume control. Years ago, as a young college graduate, I had the privilege of knowing an old, godly preacher from the mountains of Tennessee. He was a BIG man with BIG hands. Occasionally, when he wanted to emphasize a certain point, he would turn up the volume and slap those big hands together. Sounded a little like thunder. Being young and impressionable, I thought that was a neat idea that I could use in my teaching. Well, one day during a class I felt it was a good time to use this teaching strategy, so in making some point, I cranked up the volume and slapped my hands (considerably smaller than those of my role model). One big problem. There was a very sweet, shy young lady sitting on the row right in front of me. She nearly jumped out of her skin! So unless you want to be guilty of triggering a cardiac arrest in your class, you might want to forget the idea of the hands and just raise the volume. Sometimes, if you have a microphone with a large class, you might try briefly lowering your voice almost to a whisper. Caution: with or without a microphone, don't mumble your words or drop your voice too low, which will shut down your communication with those sitting in the back of the room. If you begin to get complaints that your voice is not being heard by some of your members, try this suggestion. Select one of your adults to serve as your "VA" (Volume Assistant), who will sit in the back row, and raise a hand if you cannot be heard there. With that signal you can learn to adjust your volume.

2. Vary your rate. Those of you who speak at a rapid clip will need occasionally to slow it down. Those of you who need two minutes just to say your name will need to discipline yourself periodically to speak a bit faster.

3. Occasionally, just pause and say nothing for a few seconds. This will probably get the attention of most of your adults, providing they are not already asleep. Some may even look up just to see if you had a stroke!

DEFINITELY QUOTABLE:

"Some open minds need to be closed down for repair." (sign on a bulletin board)

"Blessed are they who have nothing to say and who cannot be persuaded to say it." James Russell Lowell

"Keep your words sweet. You may have to eat them." Stephan Grellet

STRIKE THE MATCH:

If you have a problem with being monotone, you need to operate on it and try to get rid of it. Use some of the ideas listed above or any ideas you can find that might help you, at least temporarily, to break out of this mold. Even if you are not a monotone, you can still become more effective in your teaching if you will work on some variety in your volume and rate of speech. And don't forget to use that pause. It works.

MATCH

22

USE PLENTY OF POSITIVE REINFORCEMENT

She would always sit on the back row of my classes. She was a bright, intelligent student, but never raised her hand to ask a question or become involved in any of our class discussions. Without trying to embarrass her, I used every trick in my teaching bag to draw her out of her shell and get her to participate in class, but nothing worked. Not even a holy grunt. I had just about thrown in the towel, and then one day, it happened! I can still see it now. Very slowly and cautiously her hand went up to ask a question. I felt like singing the Hallelujah chorus! Needless to say, I did everything I could at that time to provide positive reinforcement for her response.

What is positive reinforcement? In the context of teaching, it works something like this. As the teacher you ask a question or make some point that invites a reply. This has been termed a stimulus. If the student replies, this is known as a response. Your public affirmation of that response is known as positive reinforcement. In this day when so many people, even God's people, suffer from low self-esteem, it is very important that you verbally reward your adults' efforts to participate in class. But if you do this, don't give the impression that you are giving out treats to your dog for doing some clever trick. Here are some suggestions as to how you might give some appropriate, positive reinforcement to your adults when they answer a question correctly or make some type of constructive contribution in class.

1. Smile approvingly at them.

2. Immediately follow their answers with responses such as these:

> "That's great!"
> "That's good!"
> "Great idea!"
> "That's a good point!"
> "I really appreciate the work you are doing."
> "Good thinking!"
> "Very creative!"
> "Exactly right!"
> "Super!"

3. If at all possible, incorporate their contributions into your lesson.

Now notice the preceding list deals with affirming the correct responses of your adults. What do you do with the incorrect response? Suppose the response was not in the ball park. Actually, it was not even in the league! At this point you may be tempted to reply something like this, "John, are you brain dead? You could have stayed up all last night and not thought of an answer more stupid than that one." Well, if that temptation shows up, flee. The last thing you want to do in a situation like this is to embarrass your adults, for if you do, you may as well forget about them trying to answer another question in your class. In fact, they may even drop out of your class. Here are a couple of suggestions that have worked for me when handling the incorrect answer.

1. Be sure the answer is not your fault. The problem may be that your question was so vague, the person really did not understand it. If you suspect that this may be so, say something like this, "O.K., let me rephrase that question . . ."

2. Show your appreciation for attempts to participate with responses such as these:

> "O.K., that's a good point. Do you want to sharpen that up a bit for me?"
> "Well, that's not exactly what I had in mind"
> "Anyone else want to help us out here?"
> "Hey, your point is as valid as mine, but let me suggest this. . ."
> "That's an interesting perspective; I never thought of it that way before."

3. If at all possible, incorporate their contributions into your lesson.

DEFINITELY QUOTABLE:

"Nothing improves a person's hearing as quickly as praise."

STRIKE THE MATCH:

Before you teach next time, look over this section again, and look for opportunities to provide some positive reinforcement for your adults.

MATCH

23

SPRINKLE IN SOME HUMOR

Billy Sunday purportedly once said to an audience, "God must have had a sense of humor or He wouldn't have made the monkeys and some of you people." I definitely would not recommend that you try that with your adults. Yet, a sense of humor is a fantastic asset. I feel sorry for anyone who does not have a sense of humor. I feel even more sorry for the person married to someone with no sense of humor. I am reminded of what Amy Carmichael, distinguished missionary to India, once said, "A missionary needs two things: a good sense of humor, and no sense of smell." Now, when mentioning this "match" I am not suggesting that you try to become the class clown or develop the obnoxious habit of constantly trying to top other people's jokes with one of your own. However, I believe that having a sense of humor can make us more winsome and effective in influencing others for the Lord.

Several years ago, we distributed a survey to church teens (ages 13-17), asking them to think of the adults whom they personally knew, admired, and respected (parents, pastors, youth leaders, teachers, etc.). We were interested in the reasons for this admiration and respect, so we presented a list of 34 characteristics and asked the teens to check all the items they felt applied to these adults. We received back responses from 486 teens from 26 churches. We totaled the number of teens responding to each item and translated that number into a percentage of the total group. Percentages were rounded off to the nearest whole number and then ranked according to frequency of choice. Only the top five choices are shown below.

1. Has a sense of humor, likes to have fun...96%
2. Is honest...94%
3. Is easy to talk to...92%
4. Is willing to listen to me...91%
5. Loves the Lord...90%

It is interesting to note that 96% of these teens indicated that a sense of humor was a factor in evoking their admiration and respect for adults. I have a suspicion that a similar survey given to adults would find a sense of humor very close to the top of the list, for it has been my experience that adults who still have their emotional and physical health regardless of their age love to laugh and have fun. Consequently, if we want to minister to the whole person, we need to find some way to inject humor into our teaching. Let me make a few suggestions.

1. Jokes (Don't be guilty of overkill here; a few of these will probably go a long way.)
2. Cartoons. You have a couple of options in locating these. You can find them in books of cartoons and in some periodicals. Or you can make your own, either by drawing them freehand (if you have some artistic ability) or generating them on your computer with some of the clip art software available today. Regardless of where you find cartoons, you will need to convert them to some form that can be readily seen by your class, either burning an overhead transparency or putting them on a PowerPoint slide.
3. Funny stories (Again, don't overuse these.)
4. Funny quotations. Here are some of my favorites.

"Life is uncertain. Eat dessert first." (Ernestine Ulmer)
"A clear conscience is usually the sign of a bad memory." (Stephen Wright)
"Grandchildren are God's rewards for not strangling your children." (sign on the wall of a restaurant)
"A balanced diet is a cheeseburger in each hand."
"Be nice to your kids. They will be choosing your nursing home." (bumper sticker)
"Ignorance is curable; stupidity is terminal."
"Some people are a blessing wherever they go; others are a blessing whenever they go."

"Behind every successful man stands a proud wife and a surprised mother-in-law." (Brooks Hayes)

"Nonchalance is the ability to look like an owl when you just acted like a donkey." (Our Daily Bread)

"To protect your teeth, see your dentist twice a year . . . and mind your own business."

"An oak tree is just a little nut who held his ground." (Our Daily Bread)

"Always try to drive so that your license will expire before you do."

"Committee - a group of men who keep minutes and waste hours." (Milton Berle)

Summarily, the frequent use of humor in your teaching is just as important as using other types of illustrations. It enables you to gain and sustain attention, to illustrate a point or truth, and to speak to the emotional side of your adults, specifically helping them to laugh and enjoy your class.

DEFINITELY QUOTABLE:

"The best way to keep from losing face is to keep the bottom part of it shut."

STRIKE THE MATCH:

If you are not accustomed to doing this (and even if you are), find one or two cartoons, relative to your lesson, and use them next time you teach your adults. I think you will like the results.

MATCH

24

TERMINATE THOSE MANNERISMS

Apparently the evangelist was convinced that his pants were falling off, for all during his message, he would repeatedly reach down and pull them up higher on his hips. Maybe he was a successful dieter. I'm not sure. But I am sure of this. He needed to put a new notch in his belt or get some new pants. This type of action is known as a mannerism. It could be defined as a peculiarity of action or something a speaker does or says repeatedly, that tends to distract the listeners. Note that, first of all, it can be something a speaker does. Here are a few examples.

1. A preacher periodically touches the knot of his tie, as if to be sure it is still there.
2. A graduate school teacher frequently runs his fore finger across the bottom of his nostrils. Most of the time he would do this in one direction, but occasionally he would go back the other way.
3. A Sunday school teacher is constantly taking off and putting back on her glasses. Now in all fairness, this could be justified if that teacher is near-sighted and can read her Bible without her glasses, yet needs to put them back on in order to see her pupils. But if you are doing this because it's a vanity thing, get over it!
4. A speaker clears his throat repeatedly. Possibly a sinus problem? If so, get some medication pronto!
5. A teacher periodically pushes her glasses up on her nose (the longer the nose, the longer it requires to perform this delicate operation).
6. A Sunday school teacher taps his pen on the lectern with the steady

rhythm of a redhead woodpecker.
7. A teacher, usually a man, has ninety-seven cents in his pocket, and is able to thrust his hand into that pocket and jangle those coins fifty-two times in the course of a thirty-minute lesson. I am not really sure of the reason for this action. It could be some form of compulsive behavior or perhaps some type of subliminal message requesting financial aid from his class.

Then as noted above, a mannerism may not only be something the speaker does. It may also be something he says. Let me share several examples.

1. A preacher, in his thirty minute message, uses the expression, "You know" seventy times. One person actually counted them.
2. A teacher during the course of his lesson, repeatedly punctuates his points with the expression, "Uh . . . uh . . . uh."
3. A youth leader, over the course of his lesson, incessantly asks the rhetorical question, "O.K.? O.K.? O.K.?"
4. A missionary, during his report to a supporting church, constantly uses his pet word, "Exciting . . . Exciting . . . Exciting."
5. A teacher constantly asks his class, "You know what I mean?"

Now these illustrations have not been given as a criticism of these individuals, most of whom I am sure love the Lord and are trying to serve Him faithfully. They are mentioned only to make the point, no matter how well-intentioned teachers may be, mannerisms such as these will unfortunately distract their listeners and to an extent, hinder the effectiveness of their ministry. From your observation of pastors and teachers, you could probably add some other illustrations to the list above.

What are the results of using mannerisms such as these in your teaching? Worst case scenario. Some of your adults may become so distracted that they disconnect from your lesson and spend the rest of the class period watching, listening, and maybe even counting, the number of times your repetitious behavior shows up. Best case scenario. Some of your adults really try to listen to you, but their attention span is constantly being short circuited by your actions and/or words.

Solution? First, it may be that some of you have a mannerism and do not realize it. If that be the case, for your students' sake, you need to become aware of it as soon as possible. This situation can be remedied fairly easily in a couple of ways. Ask a friend (who may not be one after this experiment) to watch you teach and point out to you any mannerisms observed. If you are married, your spouse will probably provide this service free of charge. But in my opinion, the best way to discover those pesky mannerisms is to have someone videotape you teaching a lesson. And when you view the playback, behold, there they are! All the dumb, repetitive things you say and do, all in living color. Warning. If you do this, you may not like what you see. In fact, you may just resign your teaching position and look for another job!

O.K., so now you recognize that you have one or more mannerisms, either something you do or say frequently while you are teaching. Where do you go from here? Several suggestions. Go back to that friend and make yourself accountable to him. Ask him to continue monitoring your teaching and remind you every time that weird mannerism shows up. Second, go back and watch that video again (and again, if necessary). Third, make a commitment to "terminate those mannerisms" and overcome this problem. It definitely wouldn't hurt to ask the Lord for His help, because if you don't successfully get rid of these distracting habits, they are going to handicap seriously your effectiveness as a teacher.

DEFINITELY QUOTABLE:

"*Experience is that marvelous thing that enables you to recognize a mistake when you make it again.*" Franklin P. Jones

"*A closed mouth gathers no foot.*" Stefan Posthuma

"*It is better to keep your mouth shut and appear stupid, than to open it and remove all doubt.*" Mark Twain

STRIKE THE MATCH:

If you have never done this before, ask someone to use a camcorder to tape one of your lessons. Later get alone and view the playback. If any mannerisms show up (and if you are part of the human race, they probably will), make a conscious effort to eliminate them from your teaching in the future.

MATCH 25

BE ENTHUSIASTIC

If you are a NFL addict, I'm sure you have had this experience. It is January and time for the playoffs. You tune in on TV to a home game being played by the Packers or Patriots. It is 10 degrees there and snowing at kick-off time. The sideline camera is panning the crowd, and there they are. About half way up in the stands there are four to five men with no shirts. They are wearing wigs and sporting faces and chests painted with some weird colors. They are screaming support for their team and maybe waving signs. Then later, if the home team wins the game, the cameras will pan the excited fans going wild in the stands, the team's players smiling and hugging each other, and finally a camera zeros in on the comments of the winning coach. But you know what is ironic? One minute after that game is over, it becomes a couple of pages of statistics, and a few weeks later, to most of those who viewed it, it has lost much of its importance, becoming at best a very hazy memory. To demonstrate my point, in spite of all the media hype and millions spent on commercials, how many of you NFL fans reading this right now can remember who won each of the last three Super Bowls? Actually, we probably remember some of those zany commercials long after we have forgotten the final score. All of this was brought into focus for me years ago by a sportswriter, recounting the victory of the then Los Angeles Rams over the Minnesota Vikings in a 1974 play-off game, in which the Rams won 14 to 10. As an aside to reporting the outcome of the game, the writer mentioned an incident that took place at the end of the game. Ken Geddes had played the entire game at linebacker for the Rams. After his team had gone to the locker room, Geddes received a phone call, informing him that his father had died that day. The writer went on to relate how his team mates, one by one, quietly slipped into the room, trying to comfort the sorrowing player. And then the writer finished his story with this poignant statement, "Suddenly, this football game was much less important to all of them." Bottom line to this story? Even we Christians often get excited about things that prove, over the long haul, not to be very important; yet we seem to have difficulty getting enthusiastic over things that are really important, not only in this life but also throughout eternity.

The kind of enthusiasm I am referring to is characterized by warmth of feeling, keen interest, fervor, fire, and passion. Enthusiasm is not necessarily synonymous with being an extrovert, one who is generally outgoing, effervescent, and vivacious. Actually, being an extrovert has a downside in ministry, for there is a temptation to rely on that bubbly personality to get the job done, while neglecting prayer and the need for the Spirit's fullness. No, any believer, including the quiet, calm introvert, can demonstrate the type of enthusiasm mentioned here.

Yet, as I have observed some teachers of adults, enthusiasm is conspicuous by its absence in their classrooms. A graduate school teacher has each page of his class notes protected by a plastic cover, and they are all neatly arranged in a notebook. This arrangement gives the impression that his thoughts on the subject are pretty much embalmed for time and eternity. He arrives in class, opens his notebook, and proceeds to read, in somewhat monotone, his notes to his students. Talk about excitement. After about 10 minutes of this, his students will probably need a Valium to calm them down! Now this man is an extreme example of how not to do it, but unfortunately, there are too many teachers out there who generate about as much excitement as watching paint dry. Results of exposure to teachers like these? Mega-boredom. In this connection, I am reminded of what Jim Rayburn, founder of Young Life, once said, "It's a sin to bore a kid with the Gospel." Amen. And I would quickly add, it's a "sin" to bore anyone, regardless of their age, with God's truth.

Yet the more I reflect on the title of this section, "Be enthusiastic," I realize that those words may seem ridiculous to some of my readers, especially the shy introverts. In fact, it seems to make as much sense as trying to recruit a three-foot midget to play center for the Lakers. But I still believe enthusiasm is an essential ingredient in being an effectual teacher, and I believe that you, by God's grace, can make it happen in your classroom. The big question is how? Let me suggest a fairly simple formula. Both before and during the lesson, remind yourself constantly of three strategic truths.

1. As a teacher, you are serving the eternal Lord. One of Heaven's mysteries is why the eternal Alpha and Omega would redeem us from sin and give us the awesome privilege of serving Him. If you are a teacher, you did not just get elected or hired for the position. You were called by God to serve Him in that capacity. I find it helpful before teaching a class to remind myself of the fact that I am going into that room for one basic reason – to serve Him, the One Who loved me so much He was willing to die for me. This fact will not only help generate some enthusiasm in you but will also sustain you through some of those times of discouragement that seem to come with the territory of teaching.

2. We need to remember that we are handling God's eternal truth. Throughout history the philosophers have tried to find truth and construct a worldview that would help us interpret this universe and our role in it. Of course, the postmodern thinkers deny that such absolute truth exists. But in bold contrast to all this, God has given to us His eternal truth, revealed in that Book you hold in your hands in class. For centuries, its message of redemption has been changing lives, irrespective of their race or language, not just saving them but fashioning them into the image of His dear Son. Are you seeing God's truth changing the lives of the adults whom you teach? Perhaps a more basic question is it changing your life as a teacher? As you study the Word in your private devotions and in preparation for your classes, do you seek to avoid, or confess if necessary, sins that are mentioned? Do you seek to obey the commands you read? Do you seek to claim the promises you find there?

For example, how real is Heaven to you? Is it just one of the truths that you have given mental assent to and placed in your file on Eschatology, or is it a truth that so grips your heart, that you find yourself frequently homesick for it? In this connection, my mind brings back the face of Shelton Carpenter, who was not only a "carpenter" by name, but also one by his profession. He never had a lot of money, living in a very simple home, for years without even the convenience of indoor plumbing. But he and his wife did a tremendous job of bringing up four children to know and live for Jesus. He was a faithful Sunday school teacher in the little church I was privileged to pastor for several years. He was one of the most godly individuals I have ever known, and was one of those rare souls, who rather consistently viewed life and time from the perspective of eternity and heaven. I remember vividly that day when he was talking with me, and with his weather beaten face wreathed in a smile, said, "Brother Len, when I get to thinking about Heaven, I get so excited, I can hardly wait to get there"! It should not come as a great surprise to you that such enthusiasm spilled over into his Sunday school class. Today as I sit at this keyboard, Shelton Carpenter is enjoying his first million years in Glory with his Savior, whom he loved. May the Spirit of God so seize our hearts with the truth of God that it will generate a similar type of enthusiasm in our classes.

3. We need to remember we are dealing with eternal souls. Those faces we see in our classes are not just connected to those bodies, but represent souls who are going to spend eternity somewhere, either in Heaven or Hell. To a certain extent, our ability to communicate God's truth to them will have an impact not only upon the unsaved adults who need to accept Jesus as Savior, but also upon the Christian adults, who need to make Him Lord of their lives. Surely this sobering fact should make us more aware of the seriousness of our task and fuel an enthusiasm to be more faithful in our teaching.

Let me close this section by describing for you an extremely effective teacher. He was a calm introvert, but he managed to exhibit a quiet enthusiasm that proved to be contagious to his students.

1. He loved the Lord, evidenced not only by the way he spoke about Him, but also by the way he spoke to Him in prayer.
2. He loved his students, evidenced by the way he dealt with them in class, including generous doses of gentle smiles and frequent words of encouragement.
3. He loved the Word of God, demonstrated a confidence in its authority, and had a quiet passion for helping his students understand it and walk according to its truths.

4. He demonstrated his concern for his students by being well-prepared for his classes. He did his homework and knew his material.
5. He was not ashamed to identify with the spiritual struggles of his students, being willing to share his personal battles with the flesh and the devil.

Summarily, this teacher was a mild mannered "cheer leader" who made his students want to learn and follow the example he had set before them. I think this is "do-able" for all of us, regardless of the type of personality we bring to this task.

DEFINITELY QUOTABLE

(two of my favorites from the pen of Vance Havner)

"The church is so subnormal that if it ever got back to New Testament normal it would seem to people to be abnormal."

"Snowflakes are frail, but if enough of them stick together, they can stop traffic."

STRIKE THE MATCH:

As you do a personal inventory of your teaching, are you demonstrating in your classes the type of enthusiasm we have described above? If not, why not take this matter to the Lord in prayer, and ask Him to ignite your heart with a fresh love for Him, His truth, and those adults whom He has entrusted to your care?

MATCH

26

WATCH YOUR BODY LANGUAGE!

When thinking of the body language of public speakers, including pastors, evangelists, and teachers, behind the lectern or pulpit, it seems that too many of them fall into one or more of the following categories. It might be helpful just to look briefly at each of these.

1. The Talking Statue. About the only things moving in this speaker are the eyes and the mouth. The rest of the body parts are basically motionless. The advantages include a definite conservation of the speaker's energy. The disadvantages, however, include casting an almost hypnotic spell over the listeners.

2. The Drugged Octopus. This speaker gives the distinct impression of being overdosed on a strong barbiturate. Constant "draping" over the lectern seems to indicate that it is the only barrier preventing a total collapse to the floor.

3. The Pendulum. This speaker is continually swaying from side to side, somewhat similar to the pendulum of a grandfather clock. Advantages include giving the listeners a "moving target," but the downside again is the danger of hypnotizing the audience.

4. The Rocker. Not to be outdone by the preceding speaker, this one also demonstrates a type of pendulum movement, but rather than moving laterally, he rocks back and forward from point A near the

lectern to point B away from it, giving the distinct impression that both legs are attached to the feet with hinges. Since the distance between points A and B is necessarily limited, it is difficult, if you happen to be counting, to keep a precise record of the number of times this maneuver is executed during a lesson.

5. The Lateral Yo-Yo. Unlike the yo-yo some of you once played with, which moved up and down, this type of speaker may move from two to ten feet to his right, then retreat and go the same distance the left, and then go back and retrace his steps in the other direction. I have not known of any instances where this type of action has induced motion sickness in the speaker, but it has certainly induced distraction in the listeners.

6. The Spastic Windmill. Now while meaningful gestures can be very helpful in emphasizing a point, this speaker tends to wildly flail the arms like a windmill out of control. This will probably not accomplish much more than the creation of a small breeze to cool the adults on the front row.

7. The Magnetized. Almost as if drawn by some gigantic, unseen magnet, every time this speaker moves away from the lectern or pulpit, the direction is always to the same side of the room.

8. The Caged Lion. Somewhat similar to a hungry lion locked in a cage, this speaker will incessantly pace from one side of the room to the other. Advantages to the speaker include a great opportunity to walk and exercise the heart. Disadvantages probably include a major annoyance to the listeners.

9. The Elevator. This species is somewhat rare, but when it is observed, it is generally found in a church sanctuary or any room that has a raised platform with steps in front. One preacher I saw recently was a classic example. Soon after the beginning of his sermon he walked to the left of the pulpit, went down one step and spoke for about one minute at this elevation. Then while continuing to speak he retraced his steps, circled behind the pulpit to the right side, went down one step, and spoke for about a minute at that location. At that point he retraced his route to the left of the pulpit and kept up this cycle for

almost the entire sermon. Although he preached a great message, I had a rough time staying focused on it because my brain insisted on following him up and down those steps.

Now, although you need to avoid like the plague the problems associated with the preceding caricatures, you must not go to the other extreme and give the distinct impression that a huge piece of velcro has you stuck to the lectern. You certainly need to exhibit some movement. While there are good teachers, on the undergraduate and graduate levels, who sit behind the desk when teaching, probably most teachers prefer to stand behind the lectern. If you choose to stand there, do not be afraid to occasionally move out from behind it and walk across the front of the room, while you continue to talk. If your class is not too large, and there is a center aisle, you might even walk to the back of the room as you continue to teach. I picked up this idea from a gifted teacher, who used to preach on the streets of New York City. It does help sustain your adults' attention, especially those who appear to be on the verge of slipping into a state of unconsciousness.

DEFINITELY QUOTABLE:

"A Christian is like a good watch. He has an open face, busy hands, is made of pure gold, is well regulated, and is full of good works." Author unknown

"The only exercise some Christians ever get is jumping to conclusions."

STRIKE THE MATCH:

If you even suspicion that your teaching style fits one or more of the caricatures shown above, or possibly something worse, get help. Just as in the case of mannerisms, already discussed, ask a friend to videotape your teaching, and make yourself accountable to that person, asking for periodic evaluations of your success in overcoming these distractive behaviors.

MATCH

27

MAKE YOUR CLASSROOM "USER-FRIENDLY"

The spacious room was carpeted, and its pastel colored walls were adorned with a mirror and beautiful, framed pictures. Its three sofas, one with a coffee table in front of it, and a number of comfortable chairs were flanked by attractive end tables with lamps. A nice floor lamp and pots of artificial flowers completed its decor. If it were not for a small white lectern tucked away in one side of the room, and a few folding chairs leaning against a wall, this room could have been easily mistaken for a showroom in a pricey furniture store. Actually, it was a ladies' Sunday school classroom, one of the most nicely appointed ones I have ever seen. Of course, not all teachers of adults would want a room this elaborately decorated, and even if they did, they might not have the option of doing so. For example, you would not be able to do much in fixing up your room if you had to share it with others at different times or days, such as in a college, graduate school, or even a local church, if its facilities were being also used by its Christian school during the week.

In stark contrast to the class room mentioned above, I have visited other adult classes, where the walls were drably painted and almost barren, the floors were wooden or cement, covered with vinyl, the adults sat on hardback wooden chairs or old pews, and the teacher had a small pulpit for a lectern. Not exactly the most exciting stuff to attract adults in this century.

If you and your adults have your "own" room, and have the option and the finances necessary to decorate and equip it, let me make a few suggestions you might want to consider in order to make it more "user-friendly" to adults. The list below, as you will readily discover, is targeted for an adult Sunday school class.

1. Paint the walls a cheerful color. Try to create a "homey" atmosphere by hanging curtains and putting up attractive, framed pictures on the wall. Unless your men are totally macho, they may not mind having this done also in their class. Actually, it seems that most men and women respond favorably to a pleasant learning environment.

2. Be sure there are an adequate number of electrical outlets in the room. It is extremely frustrating to arrive at the classroom ten minutes before class starts, and try to set up a piece of audio-visual equipment, only to discover two disconcerting facts: you did not think to bring an extension cord, and even if you had, the nearest electrical outlet is twenty miles away!

3. If your room is not close to kitchen facilities, put in a coffee maker, a small toaster oven, and maybe a compact refrigerator. Many adult classes like to schedule a time before class starts for refreshments, usually coffee and pastries. If you do this, enlist one or more of your members to work out a schedule, perhaps asking a different couple each month to be responsible for buying, bringing, and serving the food.

4. Purchase attractive, padded chairs that can be readily stacked. Occasionally change the way you arrange them in class. If your class is not too large, try to get away from the idea that the chairs have to be arranged in neat rows every week. This idea, according to some adults, seems to have originated with the Apostle Paul. Why not do something really wild such as placing the chairs in a circle or semi-circle. Also try to place them in such a way that most of your adults are facing away from the main entrance to your room. This will make it less distracting if some of your members must come in late or leave early.

5. If possible, use PowerPoint in your teaching. If you cannot afford to purchase your personal equipment, talk to your church or

school about buying this and making it available for you and the other teachers to use. If neither of these options will work, seek to purchase a good overhead projector, with a wide-angle head and a switch that enables you, if the lamp burns out, to flip a spare lamp into its place.

6. Install a dry erase board, large enough for you to print or draw on which can be seen by every adult in your class. Fortunately, you will discover that this board can do double duty. You can draw and print on it and, if necessary, use it as a screen for any type of projector you may be using. Because of its sheen, it will not give you as sharp an image as a regular screen. If you decide to install a pull-down screen, purchase one with a matte finish and hang it, not behind the lectern, but in the corner of the room, where it will be much easier for your class to view without trying to look around you. This could be particularly beneficial to the class if you happen to resemble the "before" picture in one of those ads for a weight-loss program.

7. Put in a small cabinet, with lock, for supplies such as dry erase markers, erasers, cleaner for your dry erase board, extra student books, etc.

8. Purchase a TV and video/DVD player. Due to the increasing popularity of DVD's there is a decreasing number or instructional materials being produced using the VHS format. There are, however, programs using either format that are still available and possibly suitable for your adults. You may also want to consider making use of some of the more informative TV programs, such as ones dealing with the Creationism-evolution debate, which you could tape and play back in segments to your class. It would be wise to check out current copyright laws before implementing this last suggestion.

9. Put in a small bookcase to contain extra Bibles and resources, such as a Bible dictionary, large concordance, Bible atlas, and perhaps a good one-volume commentary on the Bible. At times during a lesson, you may want to ask one or more of your adults to look up in these books some information pertinent to the subject you are studying and share it with the rest of the class. Being introduced to these valuable resource tools for possibly the first time, your adults will learn how to use them, not just in class but also in their individual Bible study.

10. If your room has its own thermostat/thermometer, enlist ONE of your adults to be responsible for keeping it regulated at a comfortable setting.

11. Provide, especially during the winter months, a coat rack in the back of the room, where your adults can hang their coats and jackets.

12. Mount a bulletin board and use it for the following:
    a. Announcements concerning upcoming events, both in the church and the class
    b. Current prayer letters from missionaries supported by your church
    c. Prayer requests from class members
    d. Cartoons
    e. Quotations relevant to the Christian life
    f. Birthday announcements
    g. Services offered/ services needed. Here's a neat idea I found on the bulletin board of one church I visited years ago. One section of the board was designated Services Offered. In that section, members could place 3x5 cards with information such as, "Firewood for sale; call Burton Fields at 724-5922." In the other section of that board, designated Services Needed, members could place cards with information like, "Teenage daughter looking for baby sitting jobs; call Tonya Martin at 724-1658." This is a very practical way for the body of Christ to minister to one another's needs.

13. If it is humanly possible, select a room where you will have a minimum of distractions and noise. I have been in an adult class that was situated directly beneath the Junior department. It was always interesting to hear those kids come down the hall and enter their room - a bit like a herd of elephants on a rampage. And then, of course, you want to minimize, if possible, the distractions within the room. One of the more memorable experiences of my college classes was the time a wasp or hornet (failed to get the exact breed) was loose in the room. There were about forty to fifty students in the room that morning, and it was fascinating to watch them duck and try desperately to get of the way as this creature practiced its bombing runs.

14. If you teach a College and Career class, you might want to consider one Christian educator's idea of putting in a reading rack, displaying

several of the leading Christian periodicals. He suggested that a class may even want to subscribe to these and keep only the current copies on the rack. Back issues could be given to students for personal use or sharing with their friends.

15. Finally, but very importantly, make provisions for that adult who is in need of special attention, such as a blind person (who incidentally may be accompanied by a seeing-eye dog) or an individual confined to a wheelchair. Fortunately, in recent years local building codes have required builders to make facilities wheelchair accessible, including cut curbs in the parking lot, marked parking places, ramps to entrances, wide halls and doors, lowered water fountains, and restrooms spacious enough to allow ample room for maneuvering a wheelchair. If your educational buildings were constructed prior to the introduction of these codes, you may need to encourage "the powers that be" to do some necessary renovations, such as installing ramps, widening entrances, and redesigning restrooms. Furthermore, if you can't afford the installation of an elevator in your church and don't enjoy carrying a heavy wheelchair with its occupant up and down several flights of steps, you may want to consider seriously moving some, if not all, of your adult classes down to the ground floor, with a minimum number of steps required to enter these rooms.

DEFINITELY QUOTABLE:

"A perfectionist is a man who takes infinite pains and gives them to others." Gore Vidal
"The only one who likes change is a wet baby." Mark Twain

STRIKE THE MATCH:

If your class has a room set aside only for its use, take a mental trip around it right now while you review the suggestions above. If you find some that might be helpful to your particular group of adults, prayerfully bring these ideas to their attention, and as funds are available, and they are amenable to the proposed changes, try to implement them as soon as it is feasible.

MATCH

28

KEEP UP WITH BREAKING NEWS

Have you ever had this experience? You are talking with one or two of your friends, and one of them brings up a topic such as the kidnapping of a certain child and the brutal murder of her parents, and you are absolutely clueless what they are talking about. Then you feel like the village idiot when they inform you that for the past four days, this kidnapping has been on the front page of the newspaper and a top story in most of the TV news programs. It is my firm conviction that one of the keys to being an effectual teacher (and a fairly intelligent conversationalist), is to keep up with breaking news in the world.

What do we need to know? Well, it would probably be a neat idea to know who is President of the country. Just kidding. But it would be beneficial to keep up with some of the major events that are taking place on the international scene, in our country, in our state, and in our local community. If you teach men, it would be good to know what's going on in the major sports in our country. In fact, there are also women who are very much into the sports scene. For years we had a wonderful neighbor, an octogenarian, who would spend hours before her television, watching basketball and baseball games. Now, it is not necessary to keep up with the individual statistics of each player in the NBA or NFL, but it could be useful if you knew, for example, which college basketball teams have made the Final Four, which NFL teams are playing in the Super Bowl, or which baseball teams are playing in this World Series.

Why do we need to keep up with this stuff? Let me suggest three reasons.

1. It will help you, as mentioned above, to become an intelligent conversationalist, able to make meaningful contributions in your discussions with others.
2. It will frequently enable you to use this information as a wedge of witness to an unsaved person. For example, just a little knowledge of what is currently going on in NASCAR could open the door for you to share the Gospel with a racing fan.
3. It will help you in class to address, from a Scriptural perspective, some of the critical issues, such as abortion and homosexual rights, that are being used to rip our American culture from its Biblical root system.

How do we keep up with the major breaking stories? A list of suggestions, obviously not prepared by a charter member of Mensa, should include the following: reading good news periodicals (preferably written from a Biblical world view), listening to radio news, and watching TV news shows. Of course, getting the news from much of the media in this country should carry the warning label: "Caution: liberals at work."

DEFINITELY QUOTABLE:

"Though the Christian must live in the world, he must not let the world live in him."

"Sticking your head in the sand won't make your problems go away; it will probably only clog your vision and give you a backache."

STRIKE THE MATCH:

If you recognize the importance of staying on the cutting edge of current news, but for some reason, have been failing to do so, why not review this section and seek to implement the few suggestions given.

MATCH

29

MAINTAIN A CHRISTIAN ATTITUDE WHEN OTHERS DISAGREE WITH YOU

I am reminded of the fictitious story of the young man who had just graduated from college and proudly announced to the world, "Here I am, world. I have my B.A." The world replied, "Come on out, young man, and I will teach you the rest of the alphabet." Years ago, I graduated from college with the somewhat psychotic idea that my four years of training would cause people to hang on breathlessly to everything I said, agree with it, and automatically go out and live differently. It did not take the Holy Spirit very long to give me a reality check.

The years have brought me some interesting encounters. On one occasion, after I preached what I thought was a fairly good sermon, a man came to me and said, "Could I ask you a question?" Feeling brash and confident, I replied, "Sure." That brashness and confidence lasted about five more seconds until his next question: "Why can't I stand to hear you preach?" Now, that kind of question can definitely cut your pride down to a manageable size. And then there was the time while I was serving as pastor that a man who attended our church became so angry with at me that he sent a message that he was coming after me (and I really don't think he was coming for a cup of coffee). Well, I thought to myself, things will get better in the classroom. And again the Lord had to bring me down to earth, and His tool was a men's Sunday school class, which was my privilege to teach. Very soon, I became aware that my earned doctorate did not overly impress these men. Some of them owned their own businesses. One served as an executive in a well-known evangelical mission board, and one of them was a pilot who flew transcontinental flights for an internationally known airline. When they disagreed with something I said in class, they displayed absolutely no timidity in challenging it. Well, then it was on to teaching in a Bible College. Surely, my fragile ego would be safe here. Another reality check. While my students were very kind to me and a bit more forgiving, some had no problem in letting me know when they felt something I said was "out in left field." No doubt some teacher reading this has gone through similar, painful experiences. Now, let's face it. Unless you are a total masochist, you don't really enjoy the hurt that goes along with this type of rejection of you and/or your ideas.

The question now is what should be our attitude as teachers toward those who disagree with us in class? If we are human, and our old sinful nature is still intact, we will probably experience one or more of the following reactions:

1. We feel hurt and offended.
2. We feel embarrassed because we have just been, to a certain extent, humiliated before those who theoretically were supposed to respect us as authority figures.
3. We feel defensive and possibly launch a "counter-attack" to establish the rationale for our position.
4. We feel angry, go ballistic, and "nuke" the individual(s) who dared to disagree with us. Something like this happened to a Christian college teacher I knew. He was a faithful brother and a great communicator, but one day something went badly in his class, and he "lost it." Whereupon he proceeded to rain down "fire and brimstone" on his students. But there was a happy ending to this story. Because he was basically a good Christian man, he came back later and apologized for his behavior before the entire class. Perhaps you have gone through a similar experience. During class, one of your adults challenged you or disagreed with you, and you did not handle it well. Possibly you displayed a carnal attitude and said some things you wish you could bring back. If you want to keep God's hand of blessing on your ministry, confess your sin to Him, and as soon as possible, go find that class member, and be reconciled.

To help immunize us as teachers from responses such as these, let's look at some guidelines to help us maintain a Christian attitude when our adults disagree with us, either in or out of the classroom. With the exception of the first point, they are not listed in any order of significance.

1. Choose carefully the "mountains you are willing to die on." The "mountain" where we need to dig in and be willing to die on is the mountain of the Bible, the Word of God. Within this Book are certain truths, which in the early part of the twentieth century, were termed the Fundamentals of the faith. Some of the more well-known of these Fundamentals are God's creation of the universe, the inspiration of the Scriptures, the Trinity, the Virgin Birth of Jesus, the Deity of Christ, His substitutionary death on the cross for the world, His resurrection, and His Second Coming. Such truths we believers consider to be essential to our faith and consequently non-negotiable.

2. Allow believers the right to differ with us in their interpretations of some of these truths. For example, concerning God's creation of the universe, we find Bible believers taking different positions, ranging across a continuum that includes views, such as Theistic Evolution, Progressive Creationism, and Fiat Creationism (which claims that the earth is only six to ten thousand years old). Another well-known example would be the truth of the Second Coming. Again we find believers divided over their interpretations of this doctrine. Some believe that Jesus is coming back for His saints before the Tribulation (Pre-trib view). Some believe that He is coming back somewhere near the middle of the Tribulation (Mid-trib view). Others believe He is returning at the end of the Tribulation (Post-trib view). Then there are a number of modifications within each position. Personally, I don't think we will ever get this one settled, until He actually arrives. At that point, as the saints are rising in the air, the Pre-Trib crowd will be able to tell the others, "I told you so!"

3. Allow believers the right to differ with us on a number of other questions, such as which is the most accurate version of the Bible, what type of music should we be using in our churches, or something infinitely more critical: clapping or no clapping in our services! But in all seriousness, these types of issues are currently very explosive and divisive among believers at least in some parts of our country.

4. Love believers who disagree with you. Now, you may need to spend a little time asking the Lord for help with this one, but just remember, He did command us to love other Christians. You might want to check out John 13:34, 35.

5. Pray for believers who disagree with you. I am not advocating that at the moment of confrontation, you fall on your knees before the class and intercede aloud for the one who challenged you. Yet, there will probably be those times when someone will differ with you, and perhaps even display an attitude with it. Although you might refrain from throwing a temper tantrum at the time of this rebellion, you may well afterward harbor some feelings of resentment, even hostility, toward that person. If that happens, you need to send an S.O.S. to Heaven and ask the Lord to work on your attitude. Actually can you think right now of any Christians whom you don't like to be around, in or out of class? Their personality and/or actions tend to rub you like sandpaper. Let me make a suggestion. Start praying for them daily. Your prayer might not instantly change those Christians, but it will certainly change your attitude toward them.

6. Keep in mind that there is the extremely remote possibility that you may be wrong in your view-point, and they are right. The study of any academic discipline, including Theology, must allow for human error in interpreting the facts. One graduate school professor put it something like this, "I doubt if any one system of theology has all the truth." As the years have passed, and I have been exposed to the differing positions of believers in the areas of theology and church polity, I have come to the conclusion that he may have been correct.

7. If you become convinced that you have erred, perhaps in not getting your facts right, be willing to admit it, apologize to the class for not doing your homework, and then move on.

DEFINITELY QUOTABLE:

"The more arguments you win, the fewer friends you will have." Sir Richard Burton

"It takes God a long time to get us out of the way of thinking that un-

less everyone sees as we do, they must be wrong." Oswald Chambers

"Swallowing angry words before you say them is better than having to eat them afterwards." H. Jackson Brown, Jr.

"Patience is the ability to let your light shine after your fuse has blown." Author unknown

"You'll never get rid of a bad temper by losing it." Alfred E. Neuman

"God reserves the right to bless and use someone who might disagree with you." Chuck Swindoll

STRIKE THE MATCH:

While it is relatively easy to demonstrate a Christlike spirit with your class at the beginning of your lesson, it may get a little more difficult to maintain that spirit when you start running into some opposition from some of your adults. Unfortunately, there is no simple answer to this problem, but many teachers have found the following to be helpful. Be faithful in your daily, personal devotions, keep your sins confessed, submit yourself to the control of the Holy Spirit, and prayerfully seek to follow the guidelines given above.

THE LAST LESSON

I remember it vividly. One morning years ago, as a graduate student, I was early for my first class that particular day (a rare event for me), and as I walked into the room, no one else had yet arrived. I had gone to grad school for one purpose: I felt the Lord had called me to teach in a Christian college. Well, that morning, with no one else in the room, I found myself walking around behind the professor's desk, looking out over rows of empty chairs, and dreaming of the day, Lord willing, when He would allow me to teach in a situation similar to this. In His time, He graciously made that happen and gave me the privilege of teaching and developing friendships with some of the finest men and women I have ever known. But the sobering truth is from the time I stood in that empty classroom to the present hour, the years have seemed to fly. I am reasonably sure that some of you reading this now can relate to that feeling. One of these days, we shall lay down our notes, put away our books, and teach our last lesson. Subsequent to that, either through death or the Rapture we will be ushered into the presence of the Master Teacher, Who will give us our final exam. Paul describes this event in I Corinthians 3:12-15 and later in his second letter in II Corinthians 5:10. None of us knows exactly what that exam is going to be like, but when He gives us our final grades, I'm sure that you join me in my fervent desire that His final evaluation will be, "Well done, thou good and faithful servant."

APPENDIX A:
SAMPLE PRAYER LIST

NOTE: Every Christian probably needs a prayer list where specific requests can be recorded and regularly remembered before the Throne. D.L. Moody said, "Don't trust your memory; write it down."

SUGGESTIONS

1. Use a small loose-leaf notebook or a spiral bound pad. The former is probably the better idea, since it will enable you to remove older requests (that have already been answered or no longer needed) and insert pages with new needs.
2. Encourage others to keep a prayer list, perhaps sharing with them a copy of this handout.
3. Keep adding requests to your list as needs are brought to your attention.
4. Maintain one section for pressing, current requests and cross them off as the Lord answers and meets needs.
5. Make foreign missions a large part of your list.
6. Reserve a specific section for definite answers to prayer.
7. Intersperse your prayer list with Bible promises concerning prayer. Perhaps even include one verse at the top or bottom of each page.
8. It might be good to print your name and address at front of your list.
9. Don't consider your prayer list an automatic ticket for making you an effectual prayer-warrior. Only the Holy Spirit, time, and your faithfulness can make that happen.
10. It might be a good idea to print these words on the first page of your prayer list: "The only thing that I deserve is Hell, but I come in Jesus' name. Lord, at any cost to me, teach me to pray."
11. Seek to guard against your prayer list becoming a simple ritual, "an Evangelical rosary."
12. Perhaps you might wish to keep one page in your prayer list for requests you would pray for each day, such as family members.

SAMPLE PRAYER LIST
(Make a separate page for each item under each day shown below.)

SUNDAY
    Names of members in your class
    Missionaries and ministries to Muslims
    Friends with special needs
    New converts you are seeking to disciple

MONDAY
    Missionaries and ministries in England and Europe
    Missionaries and ministries in Middle East and India
    Political leaders (President, Governor, Mayor)
    Christian ministries with a humanitarian outreach (ex. Samaritan's Purse)

TUESDAY
    Missionaries and ministries in Asia (ex. China, Korea, Japan, Thailand)
    Missionaries and ministries in Australia
    Christian radio ministries (ex. Trans World Radio, Bible Broadcasting Network)

WEDNESDAY
    Missionaries and ministries in island nations (ex. New Zealand, New Guinea)
    Missionaries and ministries in Canada

THURSDAY
    Missionaries and ministries in Mexico
    Missionaries and ministries in Central America
    Missionaries and ministries in South America

FRIDAY
    Missionaries and ministries in Africa and Madagascar
    Christian schools, colleges, and universities

SATURDAY
    Israel
    Missionaries and ministries seeking to reach Jewish people
    Ministries in America (ex. Word of Life)
    Your local church, Pastor, staff, people, and ministries

ANSWERS TO PRAYER (list)

APPENDIX B
SAMPLE LESSON PLAN (FORMAT)

Title: Date:

Scripture:

Target group: Place:

Lesson aim:

Checklist of items needed:

   I. Introduction:

   II. Outline:

   III. Review and closing application:

APPENDIX C
SAMPLE LESSON PLAN (COMPLETED)

NOTE: to help clarify (I hope) your understanding of this sample, I have used the format shown in Appendix B and used the following key:

Lesson plan outline is shown by underlining (ex. <u>Title</u>)
Methods and instructions are shown in italics (ex. *Buzz Groups*)
Lesson notes appear in regular font (ex. This sin was committed in special circumstances)
Applications shown in bold type (ex. **we also sin many times**)

<u>Title:</u> FIVE SINS AGAINST THE HOLY SPIRIT
<u>Scripture:</u> Matthew 12: 22-32
<u>Target Group:</u> Young Married Couples (Salem Baptist)   <u>Date:</u> August 24, 2003
<u>Lesson Aim:</u> That these adults both understand the types of sins against the Spirit, and if applicable to them as believers, seek His help in not yielding to them
<u>Checklist of items needed:</u> Dry erase board, marker, and handout (Appendix D)

I. <u>Introduction:</u>
Case study. Addressing John, one of your class members, "John, you are at home next Saturday, working on a minor plumbing job, and the doorbell rings. You open the door, and there are two Jehovah Witnesses standing there. Attempting to witness to them, you soon find yourself discussing doctrine, and in the course of this conversation, one of the pair states that the Holy Spirit is not a Person, but rather a kind of force, such as electricity. How would you respond to this?" *Be sure to allow John some time to answer. When you feel he has finished, you may want to invite others in the class to share their ideas.* Hopefully, out of this discussion, you will help them see that we can't lie or grieve a "force" like electricity, but we can lie to and grieve the Spirit, because He is indeed a Person, the third Person of the Trinity.

A. *If you have enough members present, divide the class into 5 Buzz Groups. If you have only 10 adults or less, use the Couple Buzzer method (see Match #16 for instructions how to use this method).*
B. *If possible, encourage the groups to arrange their chairs so they can huddle for their discussion.*
C. *Ask each group to select a leader to guide their discussion.*
D. *Distribute your handouts and be sure each adult has a copy.*
E. *Assign to each group one of the 5 sins listed in the first column, and ask them to look up the Scripture given with it, and any related Scriptures, find the information requested concerning that particular sin, and write down their findings in the 4 spaces to the right.*
F. *Allow about 15 minutes for this, and then call them back together.*
G. *Inform group leaders that they should be ready to report their group's findings when you call on them.*

II. <u>Lesson Outline:</u>

NOTE: AS YOU WORK YOUR WAY DOWN THROUGH THIS OUTLINE, IT IS VERY IMPORTANT THAT AS YOU COME TO EACH SIN AND MOVE ACROSS THE COLUMNS TO THE RIGHT, YOU STOP AT EACH COLUMN AND ASK THE GROUP RESPONSIBLE FOR STUDYING THAT SIN TO SHARE THEIR NOTES BEFORE YOU SHARE YOURS !!!!

A. Sin #1 - Blasphemy against the Spirit (Matthew 12:22-32)
   1. Meaning of this sin. The word in the original has the ideas of slander, detraction, speech which are injurious to another's good name, specifically, impious and reproachful to God. Two possible interpretations are as follows:
      a. This sin was committed in a special set of circumstances (during life of Christ) and, therefore, will never again be replicated.
      b. This refers to the unsaved person's final rejection of the work of the Holy Spirit, the only One Who can bring us to God and His forgiveness. Obviously your personal choice of these interpretations (or any other one) is going to influence how you respond to the other questions. Just to demonstrate how this would work, let me suggest that the correct answer is letter "a" above. If that's not your choice, PLEASE don't trash the book. Just forgive me and keep reading!
   2. Who can commit this sin. Since the context shows the Pharisees guilty of this sin, we probably can safely conclude that only the unsaved (specifically, those in Jesus' day) were capable of doing this.
   3. Ways to commit this sin. In this context, their sin seems to be attributing the miracles of Christ to the work of the devil.
   4. Consequences of committing this sin. Having rejected the work of the Spirit, Who alone can bring us to Christ and salvation, these Pharisees would have died and gone to Hell. Incidentally, if anyone is anxious over whether or not (s)he has committed this sin, that anxiety is probably a good indicator that they have not.

B. Sin #2 - Resisting the Spirit (Acts 7:51)
   1. Meaning of this sin. The word has several meanings:
      a. to fall upon, run against
      b. to be adverse, oppose, strive against.
   2. Who can commit this sin. In this context, unsaved Jews, both their ancestors and that present generation, seem to be the ones who had been guilty of this sin. And yet, given the meaning of the word, "resist," it would seem likely that unsaved persons, ever since Stephen's time, have been guilty of resisting the work of the Spirit as He has sought to bring them to conviction and faith in Christ.
   3. Ways to commit this sin. Those unsaved Jews in Stephen's day resisted the Spirit by rejecting both the Word of God and the Son of God. Unsaved persons today can commit this sin in a number of ways: throwing down a Gospel tract given to them, changing the TV or radio stations whenever they recognize a Gospel program being aired, or sitting through any presentation of the Gospel and refusing the invitation to come to Christ.

4. Consequences of committing this sin. Because those Jews resisted the Spirit, they were lost and went to hell. Those consequences are tragically still true today.

APPLICATION: It is sobering to realize that it is possible for someone to attend this church for years and hear the Gospel but resist the gentle invitation of the Spirit, and one day die and go out into eternity without Christ. If there is any doubt in your mind about your being saved, please come and talk to me, and you could settle this matter today.

C. Sin # 3 - Lying to the Spirit (Acts 5-3, 4)
  1. Meaning of this sin. The word can mean:
     a. To lie with a conscious and intentional falsehood
     b. To deceive.
        In the context of this passage, Ananias and his wife Sapphira cooked up a scheme to deceive the church by saying that the money they had brought to the church represented the entire amount they had earned through the sale of their property. It is interesting that Peter, in his confronting of the pair over their sin, says in verse 3 that they had lied to the Holy Spirit, and later in verse 4, he says they had lied to God, another confirmation of both the personality and the Deity of the Spirit.
  2. Who can commit this sin. Determining whether Christians and/or unsaved can commit this particular sin is going to be difficult for at least two reasons: (1) it is not clear from the passage whether Ananias and Sapphira were actually saved or just counterfeits similar to many occupying our church pews today, and (2) this is the only place in the New Testament where this expression is found. If, however, this sin can be called lying to God, as Peter seems to indicate in 5:4, then we Christians can surely be guilty of this one.
  3. Ways to commit this sin.
     Question: "How could we Christians today be guilty of lying to God?"
     Address this first to the group who researched it, and then possibly open it up to the rest of the class for their suggestions. Encourage members to take notes. After this time of discussion, you may want to share some of the following ideas:

APPLICATION: Many times we lie to God when we get stuck with the consequences of some stupid sin and promise Him we will never do it again, when in reality we just want to get out of the mess we created and have no intention of repenting and forsaking the sin. Most of us do an incredible job of lying (hopefully not intentionally) to God at church during the song service. We sing out with gusto, "I love to tell the story", and we can't remember the last time we handed out a Gospel tract or tried to lead someone to Jesus. We sing, "Sweet hour of prayer," and we talk to Him about five minutes, if that much, each day. We sing, "I surrender all" and refuse to give Him even the tithe of our paycheck. I could go on, but I think

you probably get the point.

    4. Consequences of committing this sin. In the case of Ananias and Sapphira, the consequences were pretty radical.

    APPLICATION: It's probably good that the Lord is a bit more lenient with us in church today, or we would be scheduling funerals for church members fairly regularly. And while we cannot predict with much accuracy the actual consequences we will experience when we lie to God, I think it is safe to say that such sin still grieves our Lord, hinders our usefulness for Him, and may possibly bring His chastening hand into our lives.

D. Sin # 4 - Quenching the Spirit (I Thessalonians 5:19)
    1. Meaning of this sin. The verb here has several meanings:
        a. To extinguish
        b. To hinder
        c. To thwart
        Literally, it can mean to quench, like extinguishing a fire. Figuratively, it seems to mean to extinguish another's voice, i.e., disobey.
    2. Who can commit this sin. The context indicates that Paul here is warning believers.
    3. Ways to commit this sin.

BRAINSTORM: Ask class members for ways we can quench or disobey the Spirit. List their contributions on the dry erase board. When they have finished, add any of your own ideas they may not have included.

APPLICATION: Examples of how we can quench or disobey the Spirit might include the following: (1) The Spirit rebukes you for your harsh words to your wife and tells you to ask her forgiveness, but you are too stubborn to admit to her that you were wrong, (2) The Spirit speaks to your heart about witnessing to your doctor, but you somehow feel intimidated by him and fail to do so (3) You have a sharp disagreement with another church member and refuse to talk to him, even avoiding him by walking down a different aisle in church. The Spirit says to go and ask his forgiveness, but again you refuse to obey Him, because you're too proud to admit you were wrong.

    4. Consequences of committing this sin.

APPLICATION: As in the case of any sin in the believer's life, if we allow it to remain unconfessed, it will grieve our Lord, rob us of our joy and peace, and short circuit the flow of the Spirit's power in our lives and ministry. On the other hand, repentance and confession of sin, to God first, and others when necessary, have frequently resulted in His bringing genuine revival in our churches and schools.

E. Sin # 5 - Grieving the Spirit (Ephesians 4:30)
1. Meaning of this sin. This verb also has several meanings:
   a. To make sorrowful and to affect with sadness
   b. To grieve
   c. To offend
   As mentioned earlier, this is a powerful proof text for the personality of the Spirit, Whom we can grieve and sadden by our actions.
2. Who can commit this sin. In the context, it is clear that Paul is referring to believers.
3. Ways to commit this sin.

BRAINSTORM: Ask class members to list ways we as Christians can grieve the Spirit, encouraging them to check out the context of this verse (vss. 25-32). Record their contributions on the board, adding any others you feel are relevant.

APPLICATION: From Ephesians 4:25-32, we could conclude that some of the sins that might grieve the Spirit would be as follows:
   a. Lying (example: choosing not to report a certain amount of your income in your tax return)
   b. Anger (example: losing your temper when a driver cuts in front of you on the highway or into a parking place when you arrive there first)
   c. Stealing (example: failing to return the money when a clerk gives you too much change after you make a purchase)

4. Consequences of committing this sin.

APPLICATION: Years ago, it was brought to my attention that our sins, as believers, many times hurt ourselves and others, but always hurt and grieve our Lord

III. Review:

In this lesson, we have looked at some of the sins against the Spirit including: blasphemy against Him (only possible for the unsaved to commit), resisting Him, lying to Him, quenching Him, and grieving Him. From the Scriptures examined, it is clear that we as believers can be guilty of committing any of the last three sins in this list.

APPLICATION: As we close in prayer now, would you who know the Lord ask Him to show you where you have lied to, quenched, or grieved His Spirit, and when He reveals that sin to you, will you right now confess it to Him (and others, if necessary) and daily seek His help in overcoming these sins?

APPENDIX D
FIVE SINS AGAINST THE HOLY SPIRIT

Types	Meaning	Who Can Commit	Ways to Commit	Consequences
1. Blasphemy Against the Spirit Matthew 12:22-32				
2. Resisting the Spirit Acts 7:51				
3. Lying to the Spirit Acts 5:3, 4				
4. Quenching the Spirit I Thess. 5:19				
5. Grieving the Spirit Ephesians 4:30				

CPSIA information can be obtained
at www.ICGtesting.com
Printed in the USA
FFOW01n1347260416
23610FF